Sharman has created a thought-provoking template for a successful life. It's refreshing to see a successful business woman reaching out to help other women. Her words will inspire you to reach your full potential and pass it on.

—*Sunny Kobe Cook*
Award-winning Entrepreneur

Sharman Dow helps you achieve your potential with candor and forthrightness. When you apply what you have read, you are guaranteed to have an increased impact and greater personal success.

—*Devi Titus*
Author/Speaker
Vice President of Kingdom Global Ministries

This is a book every leader needs. Sharman Dow has communicated brilliantly the tools we can all use to positively transform our businesses and relationships.

—*Tammy Kling*
Author, Thought Leader, Humanitarian
Founder, The Homeless Writers and Speakers Project

It takes special insight to merge things that are timeless with things that are relevant. Because it's tough, much of life—in real time—is disconnected from the wisdom of history. Sharman Dow has connected the greatest summation of the ground rules for life with the challenges of living with integrity as a woman in the marketplace. Ponder the past and expect success without duress.

—Bob Shank
Founder/CEO, The Master's Program

TEN
COMMANDMENTS
of Business Success
for Women

Reaching Your Goals
with Integrity

SHARMAN DOW

Oviedo, Florida

The Ten Commandments of Business Success for Women—
Reaching Your Goals with Integrity

ISBN Hardback: 978-1-939183-57-6
ISBN Ebook: 978-1-939183-58-3

Published by HigherLife Development Services, Inc.
HigherLife Development Services, Inc.
400 Fontana Circle
Building 1, Suite 105
Oviedo, FL 32765
www.ahigherlife.com

Printed in the United States of America.

Table of Contents

Acknowledgments

I WOULD LIKE TO ACKNOWLEDGE those who helped me in this endeavor. Without them I could not have completed this book:

My husband, Bruce, who first had the idea that I should write a book geared toward businesswomen. It took a long time for me to take his idea and run with it, but finally, with his prodding I was able to get it done. His support and belief in me never fail!

My publisher, David Welday, and his awesome staff for their patience, support, and good editing.

Tammy Kling and Devi Titus—two awesome ladies of God who also believed in this book and were faithful and extremely creative in writing, producing graphics, and providing support. Thank you from the bottom of my heart. Also, my "Birthday Girlfriends" (Dana Liberatore, Kristine Amerson, Linda Tavani and Tammy Nestlerode) who are great prayer partners and wonderful confidants.

I know this may sound silly, but I also want to thank Moses for being faithful to the call and giving us The Ten Commandments from God. Without this foundation of right behavior, ethics, and morals, it is questionable where we might be as a society today.

Introduction

WHAT IS YOUR LEGACY? When you die, what will people say about you? What have you deposited into the lives of others that will live on? *Legacy* is that divine gift handed to you—the gift you've accepted, the life you're creating by listening to and answering your calling. It is not a slogan or phrase on your business card. No, legacy is built brick by brick, over a period of decades. Your legacy was handed to you, and it is part of what makes you so special and unique. Passing it on with integrity requires determination, persistence, and intention. Someone once said, "What matters most with your legacy is not what happens to you, but what happens through you. It is a life lived by choice, not by chance."

Much of my legacy came from the business world and my career. I discovered that what I am passionate about is helping others see the unseen, helping them understand what makes them tick, and driving success in their business and personal lives. I found I enjoy seeing others accomplish their goals so that they can become positive forces in our culture and can pass it on to the next generation. I want to do the same for you.

If you want your legacy to last and be authentic, then it needs to align with who you really are, or at least who you want to become. My heart's desire is to give you insight and vision for reflection and consideration in your own life. It is my hope you will consider small changes in your thinking in order to take giant leaps in your life. The result will be lasting fulfillment, which is what we all desire in our businesses and personal lives. A small adjustment in your thinking can have lasting impact in your destiny. It can be challenging and fun at the same time. Yes, I know life is hard, but it can be an exciting journey when you have the right tools and mindset. So let's have some fun as we travel together and consider these Ten Commandments for business and personal success.

Whether you're religious, spiritual, or have no belief at all, your life must be built on truth if you decide to become intentional about your legacy. I am building my legacy on the Ten Commandments. I believe those laws, which were delivered high on a mountain nearly 3,500 years ago, continue to provide us with a strong foundation of truth for successful living that is applicable to any society in any age.

These commandments have guided behavior in every culture and continue to serve as a moral teaching for us to follow. Those tablets have impacted generations and created appropriate behavior in civility, ethics, and morality for all of us. They continue to be a moral compass for civilization to follow. They will help establish a positive legacy for your life as they have for mine.

We've witnessed the fall of some of the greatest leaders in the world because of a lack of moral and ethical principles. You can have all the success of the world, but unless you can look at yourself in the mirror with a clean conscience, then you've lost the chance to leave a legacy of significance and true success. As I thought through the best way to pass on to you some success principles, it made sense that what I'm about to share with you should be aligned in some way with the spirit of those immortal truths in the Ten Commandments. So I developed my own set of commandments to help women develop integrity and get results in the workplace—thus the title of this book, *Ten Commandments of Business Success for Women.*

You will see parallels between the Ten Commandments in the Bible and the *Ten Commandments of Business Success for Women.* Here is a side-by-side comparison:

God's Ten Commandments	Ten Commandments of Business Success for Women
You must not have any other god but Me.	Have a single-minded focus.
You shall have no idols.	Find your passion.
You must not misuse the name of the Lord your God.	Elevate yourself.
Remember to observe the Sabbath day by keeping it holy.	Take time out.
Honor your father and your mother.	Embrace authority.
You must not murder.	Forgive and let it go.
You must not commit adultery.	Be loyal.
You must not steal.	Give of yourself.
You must not testify falsely against your neighbor.	Be authentic and truthful.
You must not covet anything that belongs to your neighbor.	Find contentment.

The purpose of this book is to help you learn to claim your legacy and pass it on to the next generation. It's something that has to be learned; I had to learn it, too. Early in my career, I used my gender to my advantage. It's not that I dressed provocatively, but I did know that being a woman gave me an advantage over my male peers, and I used it. But after stumbling a few times, I realized that there should be more to my legacy. I wanted to pass on something worthwhile to my own children, and now I want to pass it on to you.

As a successful woman in business, I'd like you to set your bar high. Women have adopted some pretty low standards over the past decade as a result of following societal behavior, television reality shows, and an overall lowering of morals. I always thought that the women's rights movement demanded equal opportunity and pay, but we women have made it a new game by challenging men's sexuality in the workplace. Are we sending the wrong message and not realizing it? Let's start changing our thinking and putting forth righteous and virtuous values in our actions instead of allowing society to dictate our behavior. Have we allowed our culture's lack of morality to desensitize our thoughts and good intentions?

It's possible that you have forgotten how to respect others, and that has made it difficult for you to be loyal to your family and friends. Do you tear down a coworker who is more successful than you just because you are jealous? Or are you the office gossip who trashes your friends on the way to the coffee room? Some women spend much of their work time visiting coworkers and wasting half the day on gossip instead of doing the work they were hired to do. Is this you? Loyalty is a virtue that can be developed, and this book will teach you how.

Some of us have problems with authority. We are so rebellious that we cannot submit to our boss's request on a project, or we usurp his or her authority and go over that person's head. I know I have done this—how about you? Or perhaps you are dealing with an inability to forgive and are bound in bitterness and resentfulness toward others. These behaviors are success blockers and will squelch your legacy and business success. Perhaps your problem is lying or bending the truth, and you've been caught a few times in your white lies. Do you justify your false truths because everyone else does it? Maybe you are a workaholic, and you don't know how to take some time off to get to know yourself. Whatever your issues are, this book will address them. It will force you to look at yourself in an honest light and help you achieve success by adopting the personal behavior of a woman of character and principle.

I wrote this book to enable each of us to examine our lives, sharpen our swords, and have a stronger finish to the race for business and personal success. Today is a new day for you. This is a book about creating an influential legacy.

Your short- and long-term success will have more to do with your legacy than you might suspect. Success isn't about a formula, a technique, or a program. It's all about determining what kind of mark you want to leave with your life.

If you were to die tomorrow, what would people say about you? Are there people in your life—family, friends, and coworkers—who have been impacted by you positively? Or are you embarrassed at what people might say about you? That's your legacy. Choose to make it count.

Commandment

Have a Single-Minded Focus

THERE IS PERHAPS NO more powerful force in the quest for success within a business profession than having a single-minded focus, which is the ability to concentrate and direct all attention to one area. It has been proven time and time again that anything you want to achieve in life will take a single-minded, concentrated effort. Any successful person will tell you that focusing his or her mind on one goal was pivotal to their success.

Athletes are focused on their goal at the expense of everything else. To compete at the highest levels, professional athletes must make extreme sacrifices, such as eating special meals, eliminating things they desire, and sacrificing time with family, friends, and loved ones to train with complete focus.

For example, Jackie Joyner–Kersee had to train her body physically and prepare her mind mentally for years to finish her races strong and win six Olympic medals. Professional golfers have to play and practice their swings regularly for years, devoting hours every day to the sport. To play the professional golf circuit, they must travel constantly and spend time away from family and friends at great sacrifice to their personal desires.

I've been blessed with immeasurable success, but it wasn't by accident. No success is. Your success will not be an accident, either; it will be the result of right thinking and hard work. The successes of others, whom you've admired or who have mentored you, were likely the result of years of learning, establishing a solid foundation, and working toward a goal. Successful people think, act, learn, and perform with a single-minded

Your success will be the result of right thinking and hard work.

focus and are open to constant personal improvement. They each have found a process that leads to their success.

But the process isn't enough. You also have to have fundamental truth, principles on which to stand, and a foundation upon which to build your life. Without those factors, no process can carry you. It might sustain you for a while, but it will eventually crumble because you haven't focused on what really matters.

Concentration Is the Key

Focus was not something that came naturally for me. Being a type A personality, I have a short attention span, and I multitask well. The advantage is that I can do many things at once; the disadvantage is that I have a hard time focusing on any one thing for any length of time. I usually get bored and want to move on to the next project. Concentration is not a skill that comes naturally for me.

I'm the type of person who has to stand in the back of a room at any seminar just to keep from falling asleep. Realizing that focus does not come naturally for me, I had to make a concerted effort to work on concentration in business matters. However, I was able to focus in sports, and I eventually learned to transfer the principle of focus from sports to my business career.

How Skydiving Taught Me to Focus

I achieved the skill of focus while learning the sport of skydiving. My father was a test pilot, so I grew up around flying. I never had a desire to learn how to fly an airplane, but I did want to learn how to skydive. It was a childhood dream of mine to learn the sport, and I would spend many hours gazing at the clouds in the sky from our rooftop. From the backyard fence, I was able to climb onto our roof without anyone knowing I was there. I used to lie on my back and watch the clouds float by, wondering what it would be like to fall through a cloud.

Years later, I had the opportunity to learn how to skydive and finally fulfill my dream of falling through a cloud. However, learning to skydive was no easy quest because I had to learn to control my fear. It truly is a mental sport. The physical part was easy, but controlling my mind took extreme measures of focus and single-mindedness. As my dad used to say, "What person in his right mind would jump out of a perfectly good airplane?" At times, while learning how to execute the right maneuvers, my body would be doing the motions, but inside I would be screaming for dear life. Fear consumed me with every jump. How could I ever overcome the inability to concentrate on the moment and cast away all fear? It was a tremendous challenge for me.

When I first learned to jump years ago, we were taught with used army gear. The sport had not developed enough to use the buddy jump (which is the current method of learning today). In a buddy jump the novice skydiver harnesses himself to a master skydiver, and they jump together. Using the antiquated and quite heavy army gear that was available at that time, it would have been impossible to do buddy jumps. When I was learning to skydive, we had to learn using a static line, just as they did in the army. Today the lightweight equipment used in skydiving makes jumping relatively easy for a novice.

Time and again, I would prepare to make a jump and wonder why I kept doing it. Doubts would blast my mind, and that familiar sickening feeling would consume the pit of my stomach. But I was determined to learn how to "fly" my body, and that determination kept me focused on my goal. Then one day, I had an epiphany while I was about to make a thirty-second delay, which means that I would make the jump, then free fall for thirty seconds. I was still in the learning stage and had worked up to free falling for thirty seconds before pulling my ripcord.

As I prepared to take my thirty-second free-fall flight, I was in the plane with another female jumper. She was calm, cool, and excited about the jump she was about to make, which was called an "accuracy jump." The accuracy she was practicing was to land on an eight-inch disc from 10,000 feet in the air. Wow, talk about focus! Can you imagine? She was jumping from more than a mile high in the sky and would be landing on a disc the size of a dinner plate. She was focused, and I was scared out of my mind. I was just hoping I wouldn't land in the onion fields near the drop zone.

We were the only two jumpers in the plane with the pilot. While she had the composure of an eagle about to make a flight, I, on the other hand, was like a chicken running around, petrified, and ready at any minute to vomit from the nauseating fear in the pit of my stomach. Watching her laugh and tell jokes with the pilot made me nervous. She was so comfortable and relaxed in her pre-skydive moment. As she departed the plane, she winked at me, gave a salute, and did a back flip off the airplane strut. I was stunned. Watching her perform the jump so casually put me on edge. How could she do it?

As I watched her disappear from the plane with such finesse, a sudden intuitive leap of understanding struck me. If she could do it, then I could, too! If she could be at ease and enjoy the ride, then what was stopping me from doing the same? It occurred to me that I was allowing fear to control me, rather than controlling the fear myself and enjoying the jump.

What a revelation this was for me! That was all I needed, and that single moment became a turning point in my thought process. That epiphany changed my life forever. Within a few jumps, I was able to maneuver my way into groups of jumpers, flying with expertise and ease as if I had been doing it for years. Shortly after, the more experienced divers invited me to join them on a large ten-man jump. I did it with such calculation and skill that all the men in the circle were shocked as I broke into the formation they had created with their locked hands. I still can visualize the stunned expressions on their faces when I showed up in their circle. It was exhilarating to finally overcome my anxiety and enjoy the sport with the boys. A few years later, it was this same group of guys who invited me to join them in some professional jumps at exhibition shows in which we jumped out of Bell Jet Ranger helicopters. It was a personal success and accomplishment to finally overcome my fear and become a professionally paid skydiver. When I first started skydiving, this was something I would never have thought possible.

When I changed my mindset and focused on the moment, flushing all fear out of my thoughts, the impossible became a reality. And it can become reality for you, too. What an eye opener this was for me! I controlled my mind and was able to accomplish what seemed to be an impossible task.

The ability to focus enables us to take our eyes off of our fears and negative thinking and gives us the capacity to accomplish our end goal. I had desperately wanted to fall through a cloud, but it would never have happened until I learned to control my fear and become an expert skydiver. It was my childhood dream, and I was determined to have the experience.

Fear was my distraction in becoming successful in skydiving. Once I learned to control my thought process and push the negative feelings of fear out, I was able to focus on each jump and accomplish the end result. Negative thinking will cause you to lose your focus and your ability to accomplish any task. Pushing all thoughts of failure out of your mind will start the process of success.

Negative thinking will cause you to lose your focus and your ability to accomplish any task.

When I finally became an expert skydiver, I had the opportunity to fall through a cloud, and what a thrill it was for me! It surpassed any expectation I ever had as a child. Falling through a thick fog, not knowing what was up and what was down, exhilarated me. I was in some sort of twilight zone. Focus and concentration kept my mind sane. I knew I would be all right once I came out of the cloud, so I kept that hope in the forefront of my mind.

I experienced how to measure the speed at which I was falling by watching my shadow against the clouds. "Fast" would not begin to explain the sensation of seeing your body fall at speeds exceeding 120 miles per hour against the backdrop of a cloud. It was so thrilling that, even at this writing, I can still feel the rush of adrenaline the experience caused in me.

Years after that skydiving experience, it came as no surprise to me, while studying the Ten Commandments, that *focus* is what God tells us to have in His very first commandment—to have no other god. He tells us to keep our minds on Him and to focus only on Him. So in our quest to obtain

> *What you focus on is what you get.*

success, as in any accomplishment we attempt, being single-mindedly focused on that one endeavor is the highest priority we can give to any project whether it is business-related, personal, or spiritual.

After I learned how to focus in sports, I later applied that focus in the corporate world. In business, it's all about focus. What you focus on is what you get. If you focus on something negative, you will get it. If you focus on something positive, you get those results.

What's Your Focus?

Has there ever been a time in your life when you really needed to focus? Maybe it was to launch a business venture, or perhaps it was to return to being the person God created you to be. Some things come naturally for us, such as riding a bike or jogging, but other things we might want to accomplish take a single-minded focus. Are you able to focus on a specific goal you want to accomplish? If not, then maybe you need to start believing you can. This is the first step you must take.

In business, decide what you want to become, then put all your energy into obtaining that goal. For instance, if it is your desire to become a lawyer, look into some night classes to get your law degree. Or maybe you want to become the top salesperson at your organization and attend its peak awards conferences. Start attending sales seminars and buying audiobooks to listen to while you are driving. You can become successful in your business by using your free time to enhance your mind. Set a goal, develop a strategy to reach that goal, and focus your attention on it daily. Even if the goal appears to be unreachable, write it out and set a plan in action to follow it. Focus your thoughts on accomplishing it every day. By taking small steps each day, you will eventually gain some ground in achieving your goal. I did this all the time in the beginning of my insurance career and even more when I started my own insurance agency.

When I first got into insurance sales, I became a generalist in all lines of insurance sales and became licensed in everything. I thought I could become a one-stop broker for all of my clients' insurance needs. However, it was not until I got focused and specialized in one area that success entered my life.

In the workplace and at home, to be focused and single-minded enables any task to get done. There is danger in a divided heart. When your time and talents are divided, you burn the candle at both ends. Anyone who has tried to juggle too much knows that and has experienced burnout or has given up, never accomplishing anything. When you begin to lose focus, life feels like a ship without a rudder. You vacillate from side to side and seek to release stress in unhealthy ways.

You can spot people who are unbalanced by the way they look and act. They tend to engage in unhealthy living, overeating, overshopping, overthinking, overdoing, overmedicating, and overconsuming. In the workplace, losing focus can be disastrous to a career! Stay focused on your goals. Finish the race strong. Be focused and single-minded.

In the corporate world, most people have specific goals. If you're a sales professional, your goals might be defined already, perhaps by a manager. But if you're an entrepreneur, it's easy to lose focus because you define your own goals, and there's always more than one thing to do.

People who own or manage their own businesses tend to have greater challenges than people who work for someone else. As an entrepreneur, maintaining focus often means finding a niche. I experienced growth in my own business when I got laser-focused on my niche. As I mentioned, I was licensed to sell all types of insurance, but it wasn't until I became focused in one area (workers' compensation) that my sales jumped, and my annual salary tripled! Then, I learned the power of focusing on one thing.

I don't think it's an accident that this is the first of the Ten Commandments God gave us in His manual for life. In the commandment to "have no other gods," He has identified Himself to be the Lord and commanded that we shall have no other gods. This has great application in business and in your personal life because the two are intertwined.

If women and men in our culture could adopt one manual for doing business, they would do well to follow the principles set forth in God's timeless commandments. We must all recognize how insightful this number one commandment is and understand the extent to which we must honor it. Are you focused on the one thing you need or want to achieve?

The book of Ecclesiastes says there is a time for everything. Keep this in mind—focus without sacrifice isn't really focus. If you are fixated on winning, you're going to have to eliminate a lot of activities that other people do. Sometimes you will even have to eliminate things that bring you joy. I faced this in my own life and business, but the rewards were tremendous.

To grow my business, I had to work ten to fifteen hours a day. Many nights, I would be the last one in the office to shut the lights off, and on many Saturday mornings I would be the only one in the office. I had to pass on a lot of fun events with friends in the first few years of growing my own agency, but the hard work produced results. I was focused and determined to build a successful agency, and I did.

> *Focus without sacrifice isn't really focus.*

Become an expert in your passion, or make your passion the area in which you are an expert. That's what it means to have clarity and focus. That's your God-given destiny or gift, and I can assure you that it's the key to every success you'll have in life from this point forward.

Questions to Ponder and Action to Take

1. Have you ever been so determined to accomplish something that it happened? How did that make you feel?

2. Do you have problems achieving clarity of focus and knowing what you really want? If so, write out the areas that are focus blockers and determine to break them down.

3. Does fear or insecurity prevent you from becoming focused on a goal? If not, what is preventing you from being focused and achieving your goal? Write it out, and create a plan of action to eliminate those obstacles.

Commandment

2

Find Your Passion

PASSION IS AN EMOTION that deeply moves you. It is an ardent fervor toward something that stirs you to action. It gives you enthusiasm about a particular interest and moves you to pursue devotion to a cause with great zeal. Passion is excitement that provides you with a steadfast source of energy to accomplish a goal. Its very existence within people allows them to change their destiny. Having a passion for something fills your innermost desires and drives you to succeed and find lasting fulfillment.

In the introduction, I asked you what your legacy is because that's what this book is about—determining how to leave a legacy with purpose and passion through your business career. For the definition of legacy, let's see what Merriam–Webster says: "Something transmitted by or received from an ancestor or predecessor or from the past." A good legacy is, by definition, a positive mark left on the world. It's far more than a reputation, which is simply how people think of you in the present. Legacy gives you a more eternal purpose and cause. It's what you leave behind for your family, friends, colleagues, and the world. Often, a legacy is that for which a person is most well-known, and it is guided by their passion. But because many people do not identify a purpose or a passion in their lives, their legacy is left somewhere in the clouds, floating away as time passes. It is essential for each of us to be more resolute about establishing who we are and for what purpose we are living.

Do you know what your passion is?

I'm not just talking about your career, the job you're in now, or a particular trade. Your passion is that special plan that will lead you in life and business. It's what gets you up in the morning with excitement for each new day. It's not just what you are doing for work or for your family, although these things can be part of it. It's what you were meant to do. It's the purpose for which you were made. Do you know what your passion is?

Recently, Barbara Walters retired from television. In her final episode of "The View," her daily show, almost every female television broadcast anchor appeared on the show to give a farewell tribute and visit this remarkable woman. In her statement to the audience at the end of the show, Barbara said, "These women are my legacy." Sixty years earlier, Barbara Walters had found her passion in broadcast news, and it became her legacy. She broke ground for women in broadcast news and in doing so led the way for hundreds of other women to follow. If she can do it, so can you!

You Can Be Anything You Want to Be

In this world you can be many things: a parent, a business owner, a sales professional, a news broadcaster, a doctor, an actor, a lawyer, or a dancer. Your passion can be found in any and all of these pursuits. We all have diverse interests. And today, more than ever, anything is possible! The color of your skin or your family's financial background doesn't matter. Race and status aren't issues or concerns anymore. America elected its first black president who was raised by a single mom. It also doesn't matter if you're male or female. Other countries have female leaders, and many companies have female CEOs. Women make up more than fifty percent of the workforce today, and many are in jobs traditionally held by men. Today, you can be anything you want to be.

General Motors, Yahoo, DuPont, and PepsiCo are among the major companies run by women today. Women CEOs lead some of the most well-known brands in the world. Meg Whitman, a strong and prominent fixture in the technology world, has served at Walt Disney and DreamWorks and at eBay as its CEO.

Age is no longer an issue, either. Younger people are getting into the mix with some in their twenties founding major companies like Facebook. The point? Anything is possible. The sky is the limit!

> *Begin with the end in mind by knowing who you are.*

Picture what it is you want to become. Begin with the end in mind by knowing who you are. Think the process through without rationalizing why you can't achieve something. In other words, determine your purpose, plan to make it your passion, and achieve it.

An important exercise you might want to do, that will lead you in finding your passion, is to write out your dreams. This is not a goal-setting exercise. Think about your dreams. If time and money were not a concern, what would you want to accomplish and achieve with your life? Write out those dreams. Write anything that comes to mind because anything is possible. If you start to dream, you can do it.

How a New-Found Passion Changed My Life

An important life change happened to me years ago when I met a group of gentlemen through some business connections. We struck up a casual relationship that started in business, but over a period of several months, we got to know each other and became friends. Eventually, they asked me to go into partnership with them. They offered to finance me one hundred percent to start my own insurance agency in the Los Angeles area. They agreed to make me a fifty percent partner, and they said I would run the show. The business was mine to win or lose because they lived in another part of the state.

I will never forget the moment one of my soon-to-be partners made me this offer. I was driving on the I–5 freeway, and his words were so surprising that I nearly crashed my car. It was a dream I had had since I started selling insurance, but I never thought it would happen.

However, after some thought I was overwhelmed with such an offer. The task seemed too daunting and intimidating. Could I really do this? I told him I would think about it, and I decided to take some time off to weigh the changes it would make in my life. At the time, I was very successful working for someone else, but that's just it—I was working for someone else's passion.

There were many naysayers, including members of my own family. Their concern was natural. I had never done anything like this before, and they cared about my well-being. I was also single at the time, so I had no one to fall back on to support me financially if I failed. I consulted several people, but the person whose opinion impacted me the most was a successful businessman named Dick Iverson. He was a retired CEO of the American Electronics Association and had achieved much financial and personal success. I flew up to his home in Deer Valley, Utah, to spend some time skiing with his family. They were dear friends of my parents, and they welcomed me in their home to spend some time skiing and visiting with them. I threw out all of my questions and concerns to Dick, and he talked me through the decision. The bottom line, he said, was this: "If you don't take this opportunity, you will always look back and wonder what you could have done." His words haunted me, and as I flew home from Utah, I knew then that I would make the break and start my own agency. I have never regretted that decision.

That first year was quite difficult, and at times I wondered if I had made the right decision because I had to live on my savings to survive. However, as I wrote my first policy on the floor of my empty office, I knew I had my purpose, and it became my passion. Having such a passionate goal helped me stay focused through the tough times. As time went on, I furnished the office, developed a great staff, and moved every one of my clients over to

I would repeat those words out loud—"Failure is not an option"—in an attempt to motivate myself.

the new agency. After building the company from scratch, we began to gain many new clients. I was constructing an insurance empire, and failure was not an option. Often while driving, I would repeat those words out loud— "Failure is not an option"—in an attempt to motivate myself, especially during times when I felt discouraged.

Believe me, there were times discouragement played its violin in my head, repeating the negative melody. But each time, I flushed the thoughts of failure from my mind and reminded myself of my passion.

I made many mistakes during those first years, but it was an exciting and challenging time in my business career and life. I even met my future husband during that time on the golf course. We were discussing business while hitting balls at the driving range. He became one of my new clients and then asked me out on a date.

Mistakes Will Happen

Give in to the notion that mistakes will happen, but they also become opportunities to grow and learn. When you make a mistake in business, analyze the missteps that caused the error, and learn from them. Wisdom can be obtained from examining and evaluating your blunders and subsequently making right decisions. Learn to grow from your mistakes. Proverbs 3:35 says, "The wise shall inherit glory, but shame shall be the legacy of fools." Don't allow a good mistake to pass by without growing from it!

Any way you slice it, legacy means what you will leave behind. Finding your passion and purpose will produce endless opportunities for you to leave a positive mark behind. How will you be remembered? What mentoring lessons, theories, and philosophies will you pass on or leave behind to others? A foolish woman will allow life to carry her, never learning from her past mistakes, and she will change her mind or give up on a goal at any given whim. But the wise woman will determine her destiny and pursue it, no matter how many obstacles or setbacks she may encounter along the way.

> *The wise woman will determine her destiny and pursue it, no matter how many obstacles or setbacks.*

This principle reminds me of a guy who was asked to go to a strip club by one of his top clients. He said no and went home that night knowing that it would make him unpopular and that it might cause him to lose the account. But compromising his values for the sake of the client wasn't worth it to him. He stood on his principles at the risk of losing a financial gain. A week later, his client said to him, "You know, John, I really didn't want to go out that night, either, and I admired how you didn't go along with the crowd." Their relationship grew stronger than ever because the client trusted John's character and saw that he was a man of integrity.

In His second commandment, God tells us to have no idols or images built in our hearts and minds that would distract us from Him. Applying this commandment to our professional and personal lives allows us to establish a purpose and passion without distractions. Without idolizing another person, it is important for you to find someone you can look up to in your quest for success.

Finding our passion helps us to reach out to the people who will support us in our journey—people who will mentor us, people we can trust and lean on, people who will speak truth into our lives. Finding the right people to encourage us and reinforce our purpose will help us learn to trust others. Trusting another person's character means that you have confidence in what they'll do, the decisions they'll make, and how they will represent you. A woman who has built passion into her character will eventually draw others to trust her as they see her conviction and appeal. When others are able to trust you, you will emit an air of self-confidence.

Do People Know What Your Passion Is?

Are you giving people the impression that you are self-confident? In the business world, everyone is trying to get in good with the client or the boss. Are you doing so with honor and depth of character? Do people know your passion and what you are attempting to achieve in your life? When you are focused on a passion, it will energize others. They will see your excitement and want to experience it with you.

Focusing on your passion can only bring you a better reputation and a greater amount of trust from others because they will see that you believe in a bigger purpose. Being an agreeable "yes" person, going along with the crowd, or being known as the life of the party doesn't last long or bring great rewards. A woman who has built passion into her character will eventually draw others to trust her as they see her conviction and confidence.

In business, being liked or chasing dollars (building an idol) shouldn't be the goal; your goal should always be to do what is right. When your attention is based solely on financial gain, your clients and colleagues will see right through your intentions. Instead, people trust those who connect with them authentically and represent their best interests.

Think about the best relationships you've ever had. They were rooted in trust. When you set out to build a legacy of selflessness by helping others achieve the best life possible, people will be drawn to you.

In the business world this second commandment simply means that you should do what's right, take opportunities to find your purpose and passion, be fair, and do what's best for everyone involved.

Your goal should always be to do what is right.

Do you have morals and values that won't allow you to be tossed like a ship in a stormy sea when temptations arise or the pressure is on? Or do you bend and conform to others like a chameleon? Know who you are, and know your purpose. Know what makes you passionate. Despite where life takes you or whom you encounter along the way, stay firmly planted. Know how you're going to act, what your morals and values are, and what you'll stand for so that when disasters happen, you are the cool-headed, composed one to whom others turn. There will be times in your life when a crisis of belief will occur; standing firmly on your principles will help you weather the storm. Be guided by your principles—that will be a part of your legacy.

A Person with Passion

In 1924, Eric Liddell was presented with just such a crisis of faith in his desire to win an Olympic gold medal. He had originally trained for the 100-meter heat which he was favored to win. But he learned that the race was to take place on Sunday during the Olympics. His religious convictions would not allow him to perform any form of work on Sunday. This became a great concern for him and all of Britain, as their hope for a gold medal was with Eric in the 100-meter race. He would not bend or compromise his convictions and run on Sunday. That's a person of character!!

So he was placed in the 400-meter race on another day. Running was his passion but only in short sprints. Racing in the 400 meters was not his expertise. So he ran the race in an unconventional format by treating it as a sprint. There was little hope he would win the 400-meter heat because he was a sprinter, not a long-distance runner. But not only did he win the 400-meter race, his Olympic record stood for

> *Be guided by your principles—that will be a part of your legacy.*

the next twelve years. When you stand by your convictions you may not always take the prize, but you will always win.

He later became a Christian missionary to China and ultimately died in a prisoner internment camp, serving the poor people of China there. It was later found that he had had the opportunity under a prisoner exchange to leave the camp, but, instead, he gave his passage up to a pregnant woman. A movie was made about his 1924 Olympic race. It is called *Chariots of Fire*, and it won the Oscar for Best Picture that year.

> *When you stand by your convictions you may not always take the prize, but you will always win.*

I had an opportunity to study the life of Eric Liddell in depth during the making of a documentary about his life. His legacy is remarkable. Eric Liddell was a person who lived out his convictions in every aspect of his life. He is remembered by many of his generation with great love and admiration. Here we are nearly one hundred years later, still talking about him. What an awesome legacy to leave behind!

Stick to What You Do Best

To stay successful in business, stay on top of trends and technology, but don't make them your focus. You can always hire experts in the fields in which you are uneducated or unskilled. You don't have to become the expert at everything. Stick to your area of expertise, and give it your all! This is a fundamental trait of many high achievers I know; their passion drives their actions.

When I was focused on selling insurance, I always went out of my way for prospects even if they did not purchase from me. I received many referrals by creating a positive spirit of giving. People began to trust me, so they referred others to me. I even had one CFO who, in the course of ten years, changed employers three times. Each time within her first week in the new job, she would call me to provide the insurance for her new company. She did not care what the other broker could bring to her company. She knew what I stood for, had already seen me in action, and knew I would be great for her new company. That is trust! By the way, I am still the broker at some of her prior companies, too, because her replacements also trusted me.

It was not my childhood dream to go into insurance. In fact, my passion as a child was to become an actress; I loved playing the part of being someone else. However, when a few opportunities arose to take different jobs, I realized that being an actress was rather boring. On a television set one day, I watched the same scene play at least a dozen times until the director was satisfied with the take. A few other factors added to my distaste of the industry, too, and I soon became disillusioned with the whole business of becoming an actress.

I floundered for years trying to find my passion, and by happenstance I fell into insurance sales. I started to love it, particularly because I enjoy meeting new people and controlling my own time. In addition, insurance provided all sorts of opportunities intellectually and financially. Most of all, I learned to realize my worth to business owners by being their trusted advisor. The more I learned about my chosen field, the more valuable I became to my clients. It is extremely fulfilling. In addition, many of my clients have become good friends over the years.

I soon learned that, if my end goal is to serve and give back to others, I don't have to be so attached to the outcome of selling something or getting my own way. Finding your passion will come naturally when your desire is to meet the needs of others. As you focus on your passion, people will

If your passion becomes your career, you will never work a day in your life.

see your sincerity and want to do business with you. If you learn to focus on the journey, you won't be chasing just the prize. The journey is what provides the excitement.

The Value of Building Relationships

When you are comfortable in your own skin and know your passion, you will be able to develop relationships with clients and coworkers that produce long-term loyalty and friendships. Not only will you receive loyalty, but you'll give it, too! I've made long-term friendships in the business world that have lasted far beyond the deal. Sometimes it's those people whom you can call years later for advice, mentoring, or information. If you have been good to people along the way and have focused on building authentic connections, people will remember you.

Finding your passion in life will drive your success. If your passion becomes your career, you will never work a day in your life.

Questions to Ponder and Action to Take:

1. Do you have a passion for something? If so, describe it in writing and record it for your own personal clarification.

2. Has there ever been a time in your life that you would give anything to achieve a goal? What was

it, and was there something that prevented you from achieving it?

3. To what extent are you willing to sacrifice your personal time and desires to achieve a goal?

Commandment 3

Elevate Yourself

To ELEVATE YOURSELF IS to project yourself above the standards or norms of our culture and above common human shortcomings. Elevation means to be better than you were even yesterday. It is not being puffed up, arrogant, or judgmental of others; that would create pride with a haughty spirit. Rather, elevating yourself puts you in a position of self-worth, realizing you are a treasure to yourself and others. Elevating yourself is learning to strive for your best in all situations and giving excellence in all that you think, say, or do.

What was your first thought when you woke up this morning and had that first cup of coffee? Was it a relaxing, positive time to contemplate the day, or were your thoughts filled with stress and strife? Did you immediately turn on the news or search the iPad for news stories to read about the latest murder, celebrity meltdown, or tragedy? Hard to believe, but some people actually make a choice to start their day that way.

The third commandment of business success is to elevate yourself. Elevate your thoughts, activities, and values. One very important key in elevating your "self-view" is to control what goes into your mind and heart and to begin to monitor the people, places, and things with which you surround yourself. Stop spending time with the wrong people who fill your mind with negative thoughts. You've heard it said, "You are what you eat." Well, the same principle applies to changing how you think about yourself and the people with whom you associate every day.

Monitor the people, places, and things with which you surround yourself.

Romans 12:2 says, "Be transformed by the renewing of your mind." Are you renewing your mind each day with positive and constructive thoughts? Your mind is a powerful weapon that you can use to enhance your life or diminish it. We each have developed thought patterns or habits in our minds that are hard to break. We start to think a certain way, and before you know it, a negative thought plays out continually in our lives. It's time that we start to take control of those negative patterns and turn them into a confident, affirmative blueprint that will produce favorable results.

Remember, fear is a negative emotion that will prevent you from moving forward to accomplish great things in your life. Your mind will feed on fearful thoughts and build a roadblock that prevents you from making changes and moving forward. Knock down the walls of fear by repeating to yourself, "I can do it, and I am worth it."

For me, this took place when I debated about starting my own business as I mentioned earlier. The fear of failure crept into my mind so often in the beginning that I almost did not take up the challenge. Once I convinced myself I could take the challenge of starting my own business, I had to give myself pep talks to persuade my mind that I could make it work. It may seem silly, but I would stand in front of a mirror and talk out loud to myself. I had to convince my mind that failure was not an option. As time went on, I started to realize I would be successful, but unless I believed it first in my mind, it never would have happened. If you don't believe in yourself, then who will? Start today and change your thoughts into positive "Yes, I can" thoughts!

A Toxic World

Day in and day out, we are inundated with negative messages from the moment we wake until we rest our heads in the evening. In corporate America and the workplace in general, I've noticed that people desire to talk about other people. It is a part of the world system and is ingrained in each of us from birth. It's a natural part of being human. But if you are going to be different, then taking control of the tongue is essential to your success. You're not like everyone else, and you're not in high school anymore. You're distinctive, and you are making a difference. Change your negative behavior, and create thoughts that are positive.

The fact that you're reading this book right here, right now, shows that you're focused on self-improvement. Throughout the years, I've worked in various positions, at different companies, and with all types of personalities. More often than not, just by observing others, I would get to see traits I did not want to characterize my life.

Taking control of the tongue is essential to your success.

I have found that a lot of people, women in particular, have a tendency to complain about the circumstances and events in their lives. As I grew older, I realized that complaining is a form of manipulation. Think about it— when someone complains about circumstances, she is asking someone else to make her situation change as if she has no power to make the change for herself. When we complain, we are manipulating other people to take action or to feel bad about their own condition when in reality we are the problem. Stop complaining about your circumstances and start taking action. If you don't like your job, stop complaining about it, and get your résumé out to a headhunter.

People don't like to be around complainers; it creates negative energy and poisons a conversation. If you ordered a Cobb salad but received a Caesar, and you can't live with the mistake, then quietly let the waitress know. Making a scene will only further others' distaste of your company. Don't sit at the table and keep complaining that your meal is less than what you expected. Elevate yourself with class

Complaining is a form of manipulation.

and dignity. When things go in a different direction than you expected, work around the obstacles by taking positive action in a poised manner.

I recently played in a golf tournament and was teamed up with some women I knew only by acquaintance. One gal spent the entire tournament complaining about every thought in her head. She did not like her golf game, the course we were playing, or the food that was served. Not one positive statement came from her mouth. By the end of the tournament, I could not wait to get away from her. In addition, her negative spirit was manifesting itself in her face—downward lines had become etched around her mouth, making her look old beyond her years.

Don't become this type of person. Take control and retrain your mind to see only the positive in life. It will help you age more gracefully, too! By renewing your mind, you can be transformed into a positive, proactive woman whom others love to be around.

There was a time when I would go out to lunch with girls from the office, but then I grew tired of the same old thing. It seemed that gossip, rumors, and nitpicking were as standard as the luncheon menu. It made me wonder if men did it, too, or if it was only the women. Later I learned that it's just something people do without thinking. Sarcasm and gossip have become a natural part of our culture. There's even a TV series called "Gossip Girl," so this problem couldn't be any more *bona fide*.

Set Yourself Apart

One way to elevate is to set ourselves apart. What does that mean? It means that while everyone else is doing one thing, you might want to focus on taking a different path. Instead of eating lunch with the girls, run the stairs, go to the park, read a book, learn something new, take an online class, or do what I did—work through my lunch hour to get ahead. Stop putting your own needs on the back burner and losing yourself in the process just to please others. Tell your coworkers you want to try something different for that day. You are a treasure and have value, too! It's OK to be different and break from the crowd.

While driving any long distance in my car, I always have an audiobook handy to listen to while driving. Use your time wisely and elevate your learning. Involvement in life-long learning is something most successful people I know are continually doing. Reading, trying different things, and learning new skills always benefit your self-esteem and grow your mental capacity.

I have a financially successful friend who learned in his fifties how to fly a jet. He had a desire to learn to fly and started taking lessons. Shortly after, he became instrument rated and kept increasing his skills until he eventually learned to fly a jet. He loved it so much that he bought himself a jet last year, and now he flies wherever and whenever he can.

Successful people are always open to learning new things and helping others learn. Science proves that learning new skills as you age is what prevents the onset of mental diseases and aids the growth of new cells in the brain.

This third commandment of success is rooted in the biblical concept of not using the Lord's name in vain (Deuteronomy 5:11). If everyone else is being rude, crude, or vulgar, you can really set yourself apart by being a class act! Walk away when someone is telling a dirty joke or gossiping. It's a struggle sometimes because our flesh loves to hear the juicy stories about someone, and we especially want to share them with others.

We think no one will ever know if we whisper secrets, but inevitably people do find out. Sometimes we just want to fit in with the crowd and gain their attention by joining in the conversation or sharing the latest scoop on someone's life. But next time, think before breaking the trust of someone. Acknowledge how you would hate it if someone betrayed your trust. It's human nature to want to know things about others, especially if those things are negative. We are all

Set yourself apart by being a class act!

guilty of doing this, but why not start today and rise above the norm? Set a new standard for yourself. Maintain discipline in your thoughts and speech so that you can be a person who can be trusted and who values others.

This commandment is a simple one—the only situation in which we are to use God's name is to glorify Him. This commandment teaches us to revere and honor Him by using His name properly. Why not do the same for yourself and others? Start respecting yourself, your body, your mind, and your soul. Elevate yourself. Believe you are the best thing that ever happened to yourself, and think the same about others.

We are known by the company we associate with each day, so unite yourself with people of value. Friends can influence your actions and decisions. Mingling with the right crowd helps you make more positive decisions for life. Elevate your self-worth by staying close to people who are successful and principled. Apply this rule to yourself today. No matter who you are or what you believe, you can honor and revere yourself and others. Stay single-mindedly focused on your legacy, and it will happen naturally. If you see yourself and other people in your daily life as valuable human beings, instead of competitors or simply people who fill a particular position, you'll treat them with respect and gain theirs. Spend time listening to yourself. Are you elevating your speech to a higher level by using positive words that benefit others?

Stop Using Bad Language

Recently, I watched a live simulcast debate between Jon Stewart and Bill O'Reilly. Although their political dispositions were far apart, the one thing that stood out to me, other than their political views, was how each man presented himself. I like both men, but within five minutes Jon Stewart lost me with his limited and inappropriate use of the English language. He used so many four-letter words that my mind went adrift, and the point he was trying to make was lost. My opinion may disarm you or make you feel uncomfortable, but his lack of respect for me, the listener, devalued his message in my mind. If he wants to catch my attention and get me to listen to him, then he needs to skip the four-letter words. His language gives a subtle message of poor education and disrespect for people because of his inability to use the English language properly.

Find words to express yourself with class and dignity. Anyone can use a four-letter word, even a child, but people who respect themselves and others approach their conversations with poise and stateliness.

Honor Others

Maintaining reverence and honor is a lost art, so why not start to implement those qualities in your actions and thoughts today? Think of respecting others as an art that you need to develop, just as a musician needs to study music. What if you could develop honor for those around you and, as a result, make them feel incredibly valued? By putting value on others, you will assign value to yourself.

When you value people and place them first by revering them, people will be drawn to you. Proverbs 16:24 says, "Pleasant words are like a honeycomb, sweetness to the soul and health to the bones." The wisdom and essence of these words can transform your speech and rejuvenate those around you.

Here are some things to keep in mind if you want to be a poised, self-respecting person with elegance and dignity: eliminate dirty office jokes, avoid slander and gossip, and stay away from toxic people, places, and things. Fill your mind with thoughts of gratitude and appreciation that create long-term benefits for yourself and others. Transform negative thinking into positive thoughts by concentrating on happy, joyful things. Walk away from the crowd if you feel they will pull you down. And stop using four-letter words; they demean you!

This commandment helps us learn how to respect and honor others as well as ourselves. It takes confidence and courage to break from the crowd and to not allow others to impact our decisions for personal improvement. When I stopped going out to lunch with the girls and started using my lunchtime for learning and keeping up with my trade, guess what happened? My business increased, and my mindset became more positive. If you start honoring others, respecting yourself, and eliminating the negativity from your life, you'll see an amazing transformation occur.

Take it to the next level. Elevate yourself in all quadrants of your life: emotional, physical, financial, and spiritual. Make a list today, focusing on those four categories. T. D. Jakes, the founder and senior pastor of The Potter's House of Dallas which has more than 30,000 members, calls these categories "faith, family, and finances" (T. D. Jakes, *The Great Investment: Balancing Faith, Family and Finance to Build a Rich Spiritual Life.* Penguin, 2002). Whatever you want to call them, they are the whole of your being and who you are. If you wish to elevate yourself in your business, make minor yet positive changes in your personal and business life, and you'll see great rewards. Now is the time to make these changes.

Questions to Ponder and Action to Take

1. What have you done for yourself lately that you have always wanted to do? How did that make you feel?

2. Do you have a tendency to feel sorry for yourself and live in the past? Why not start using your past negative experiences to grow and change for the better? Write out your hurts and then burn them up or bury them, determining never to recall them again.

3. Do you have people in your life who bring you down? Start making a concerted effort to meet new people and elevate your friendships.

Commandment

4

Take Time Out

Taking time out means to observe a special occasion for yourself that creates freedom from anxiety or disturbance. It's taking the time to find your rhythm and renewed vigor and to create balance in your life. It's having a place to remain idle and hear your inner voice. A place to listen and know that you have value and creativity. By taking a rest or Sabbath, you learn to find who you are and for what purpose you were made in the bigger plan of life. Rest and relaxation from your day-to-day enterprises will make you more productive. It will help you reap great rewards in your energy level and creativity. It becomes a time to celebrate you.

When was the last time you took a break from life just to refresh, take a deep breath, and pause? The fourth commandment of success is to take time out. Take time away from your business so that you can take care of the business of life. The pauses in our lives do matter.

I'm not just talking about a vacation. I'm talking about a regularly scheduled time out, a time to relax and celebrate and do nothing at all at least once a week. It's during these moments that you get wisdom and understanding about your next steps. This is one of the core principles by which nearly every successful individual I've met abides—take time to truly understand what matters and to have clarity about what you do. Spend this time in self-examination and appreciate the beauty of your life.

This commandment of success is based on the Bible's fourth commandment: "Observe the Sabbath day, to keep it holy" (Deuteronomy 5:12). If our Creator, who made us and knows everything about us, made this the fourth of the Ten Commandments, then there must be something to it.

In the business landscape, this means to take time for a sacred and special place for yourself outside of the work day. It might be a technology fast or detox that requires you to leave your computer and phone at home. It might mean you actually turn off your phone for the day, or it might mean scheduling time away from the office in the middle of the week, just for yourself. It's important to rejuvenate.

Have you ever given yourself the gift of relaxation to help you recover from the stuff of everyday life? I know someone who, on her birthday every year, gives herself a gift of an all-day spa treatment and massage. Another woman I know takes a long, luxurious bath with candles around the tub once a week and tells her family to leave her alone for an hour. Each year, some businesswomen I know plan a long weekend to be together and to enjoy some girl time, away from business and family at a relaxing resort.

Take time for a sacred and special place for yourself outside of the work day.

Whether you're an employee, a manager, or a CEO, the time-outs are as critical to the business days as the management of your workload. Taking time off is critical to your health and wellness. It's a time to recharge your batteries, gain energy, and feed your mind and soul with other things that give you energy and power.

My time each morning starts with a conversation with God. I spend time early each morning in prayer, meditation, and reading the Bible. This is my time to recap and regroup my thoughts and activities for the day. It's my alone time with God, a time when I hear from Him and learn about Him. I keep a journal and write out my thoughts and scriptures that impact me. In fact, it is from this quiet time with God that I have written my books.

Someone once asked me about my favorite thing to do each day, and without hesitation, I responded, "My daily discipline." My daily discipline of spending time alone with God is rewarding and fulfilling to me. Another discipline is working out for thirty to sixty minutes three to five times a week. I keep a very busy schedule in my corporate insurance career and in following my passion to be a conference speaker and author. I have been "bi-vocational" for the past ten years, and the only way I can juggle it all is by spending time alone in my daily disciplines. I also play golf once a week with my husband and ride my bike to get outdoors.

Find something of interest that gives you a break from everyday pressures, even if it is for only half an hour each day. Exercise or take a walk. When I am on the computer for more than an hour or two, I will take a break and do some jumping jacks, walk my dogs, or walk around for a short period. Finding small breaks in the daily routine will enhance your mental and physical health.

The Birthday Girlfriends

I have a group of girlfriends who get together to celebrate one another on our birthdays. We've been doing this for the past nine years. One of our husbands termed us "The Birthday Girlfriends" because we all make it a point, no matter how busy our schedules are, to commemorate that girlfriend on her birthday. Over the years, we have started to make the effort to escape for a weekend together at least once a year because a luncheon once every month or two just isn't enough time together. The time we share has drawn us into a deeper commitment to each other and provides a time of refreshment when we can build each other up.

Find a girlfriend, and start your own birthday club. Start celebrating yourself, and find friends to help you celebrate. After all, you are worth it!

An article in *Fortune* magazine cited sports such as golf, tennis, and mountain climbing as ways top executives get away and relax. Of those who didn't exercise, music topped the list of ways to relax. Classical, country, and easy-listening music were favorites. Music has been shown to soothe the mind, body, and soul. It has healing effects and is used in hospitals and rehabilitation facilities for that reason. What are your favorite ways to relax?

Renewal and Regeneration

Some of the best ideas I have had for business came from time away from it. There's something strange about taking a vacation and feeling a distinct pull away from my business. It might be because I'm passionate about my work, but while lying on a beach in Hawaii, I gained my most creative business concepts and initiatives. When you are relaxed, great ideas flow into your mind.

Observance of the Sabbath is a condition for healthy living; it brings inner peace. The biblical root of the Sabbath and how it applies to our lives is interesting. The Sabbath is the cornerstone of Israel, and its observance brought about personal and national salvation. God intended the Sabbath to be for spiritual and physical benefit, a time to envelop our lifestyles in praise and worship of Him. However, the Pharisees attached so many rules and regulations to the Sabbath that it became an impossible burden to follow. But as Jesus states in Mark 2:27, "The Sabbath was made for man, and not man for the Sabbath." The Hebrew term for "Sabbath" is to "cease or rest." Are you taking enough time to rest from your everyday life?

Overworking Kills Creativity

Working twelve to eighteen hours a day gets old. Old, old, old! In the 1980s, during the Donald Trump and Jack Welch era, it was about working all day and all night and being the first to arrive at the office and the last to leave. However, studies have shown that the most creative people are those who take time for rest and relaxation to question and contemplate things. Your imagination is fueled with quiet time alone. During that quiet time you allow your mind to be inquisitive.

I travel a lot in my business. I have found that flying time is very relaxing for me. There are no calls to take or e-mails to write, and no one can get in touch with me. I look forward to the time alone in the air. I take a good book for reading and listen to some relaxing tunes on my iPhone. It makes an enjoyable, quiet time.

Today it's a brand-new world. The sharpest people are rested, creative, and thriving. Companies in some parts of the world give their employees a six-week sabbatical. In Europe, people take six weeks of vacation. They sail, travel, and hike, and they don't take their smartphones with them. It's a cultural difference. In America, we are lucky to take a week off at best! We value work as a high priority. It's rare to see anyone take more than a few days off. But taking a sabbatical is about nourishing the mind and body. Take time out to enjoy the success you have had as well as the success of others. When someone else is successful, honor them. At the same time, honor yourself.

God is telling us in this commandment to make one of the seven days of the week a break from our normal routine. Make that day one in which we give Him blessing and honor. By observing this commandment, we will live a healthy and prosperous life.

Balance

When you take time away from work to rest, you will find that you are less stressed and that you strike a healthier balance between work and life. Here are some things you can do to increase your personal harmony and strengthen relationships between yourself and others:

- Find a place in your home, maybe a corner that is your special place and spend time alone to unwind. Read a book, pray or meditate.

- Request respect from your family for this time, and allow them respect, too for their time alone.

- Avoid being too busy to take time for the little things in life. Maybe it's just appreciating all the wonderful things you have been blessed with.

- Take small breaks during the day to exercise, especially if you are on the computer all day.

- Spend one day a week away from your normal routine and have fun; especially if it is with your loved ones.

Questions to Ponder and Action to Take

1. When was the last time you took a vacation just to relax and do nothing? Plan your next vacation without including any sightseeing or programs.

2. Have you ever done a spa day with girlfriends to just have some girl time? If not, plan a time to do so.

3. When was the last time you tried to have some alone time with yourself to read, think, or meditate? Block off some time on your calendar to do so.

Commandment

5

Embrace Authority

To submit to authority is to yield your desires to those over you. Submitting to authority not only makes you available to others, it also requires you to defer your wishes to another's judgment and power over you. Embracing authority makes you a good steward in managing another's affairs with honor and submission. If you are able to keep balance in submitting to authority without compromising your personal integrity, the power and inner joy you will obtain can be endless. This might be the opposite of what you would expect.

The thought of embracing authority seems to go against the very grain of every thought and desire in our being. Humans, by nature, tend to think that to bend our necks for anyone goes against the value we put on our own self-worth. However, when you are found to be a good steward of another's possessions or business, you are seen as being faithful and trustworthy. A steward uses resources to her best ability for the benefit of another or the common good. If you decide to make the owner's best interest your goal, your reliance and dependability will be displayed and rewarded.

Joseph's Story

There is a fabulous story in the Bible about Joseph, the son of Jacob, who displays a mindset of honor and submission. Although Joseph's unusual circumstances began with betrayal and jealousy among his brothers through no fault of his own, whatever position Joseph found himself in, he displayed excellence in character and distinction in service. He was elevated in whatever position he was given.

Out of jealousy, his brothers sold him off to slavery in Egypt. He quickly became the head servant in his master's household, controlling the entire estate and other slaves. When falsely accused of adultery and thrown in jail, he soon became the one prisoner whom all of the guards trusted and relied upon. Finally, when he was able to interpret Pharaoh's dream and was released from jail, he was made second in charge of all Egypt, reporting directly to Pharaoh. In that position, he managed the entire food supply within Egypt and ultimately saved both Egypt and Israel from starvation. In addition, while in his position of authority, he chose to forgive his brothers because he saw the ultimate outcome of God's plan for his life. When you honor those who have authority over you, your obedience will be rewarded, even when circumstances may seem difficult.

Even a CEO of a large corporation has to submit to the authority of a board of directors, so no matter how high up you move in your company, you still have to embrace authority. My husband is a great example of this concept. He was the CEO of his company, yet he completely submitted to his board of directors and followed their directives. He projected leadership to his staff and submitted to his board by respecting and honoring their mandates. He did it with integrity and honor, and, in doing so, earned their trust and respect.

You can't be a leader without learning to be a follower first. A leader with excellence will cast a vision for others to follow, then develop and motivate the team to follow her vision. Teamwork is about leadership support and personal accountability to the team. When you support others, you develop a strong sense of respect and community with your peers. Great leaders build and grow their team to become great leaders. They support their followers so that their followers can be the next generation of leaders.

Submission is about embracing authority instead of pushing back against it. Our natural tendency is to rebel and not submit to authority, but when we learn to submit to the leadership God places in our lives, we reap the benefits of knowledge, wisdom, and inner growth. Are you a person who can give your all to a project that benefits your manager or someone else in your life? If you can, then you are halfway to success.

Every assignment should start with the vow that you're going to do the best work on the assignment, no matter what obstacles appear in your path. This is a peaceful strategy for performing your work, and it allows you to be a team player. Most importantly, it will give you experience, as well as wisdom, to grow and become a better person. Why not look at every job or project as if you are doing it for God, not man? When we consider God as our ultimate

> *Submission is about embracing authority instead of pushing back against it.*

authority, then we will have a tendency to do a better job. Realizing that God is the one who placed our leaders over us provides an inner peace and security in working with even the most difficult bosses. By holding a place in your conscience knowing God is not only watching, but also able to guide you along the way, will change your perspective. I never hesitate to ask for His help, especially when I'm confused on what to do or frustrated by those over me. Also, thinking about Him helps me to contain my wrong choices and make a mistake that I might regret.

This fifth principle is one of the distinctions I've seen between good and great salespeople. The fifth commandment of success is to embrace authority and honor those over you. Embrace! Not just accept, reject, go along with, or put up with authority, but embrace it. To embrace means to encircle, to pull toward you, and to hug. Embrace.

If you're a strong leader, chances are that you are the authority, but we all have authority above us in some capacity. Even the business owner who is his or her own boss

Embrace authority and honor those over you.

has to answer to the client. In my business, I have to answer to my corporate manager, my support staff, and my clients. I have learned that the most effective leader is someone who demonstrates the ability to be a servant, no matter what capacity he or she holds.

I had to learn this the hard way, and it took many years in business for me to incorporate this principle into my mindset. I was always a good worker, but I never realized the importance of embracing the authority over me. And I certainly did not appreciate the importance of serving my staff and being a steward to them. In the beginning years of owning my own business, I treated others harshly in my quest to win, but what I lost was far greater than what I thought I could win. I am embarrassed to think of some of the behavior I displayed toward others. If I ever get the opportunity to apologize to them, I will.

When I finally learned to treat my staff as king, our relationship developed into one of devotion. What a transformation this caused in my business! I not only stopped to hear what was on their hearts, but I also went out of my way to give them small gifts and words of encouragement regularly. In addition, on an annual basis I invite my staff to stay in my home for the weekend, and I pamper them. I become their servant for the entire weekend to let them know how much I appreciate them. We always have a great time, but, most importantly, they leave feeling loved and appreciated. They would do anything for me. In fact, they will do things for me that they would not do for any of my peers.

When you work to develop that bond, great things can grow from it! I know several of my staff have been offered higher salaries with other companies, but they have decided to stay with our company because of how I treat them. They are devoted to me not only in business but also in friendship, just as I am devoted to them. This does not happen unless you make a concerted effort to make a difference by submitting to authority and serving others.

Value Others

This chapter is based on the business principle of embracing authority. It's in line with the biblical fifth commandment that says, "Honor your father and your mother, as the Lord your God has commanded you" (Deuteronomy 5:16).

When you honor others—your spouse, boss, clients, staff, manager, parents, children, and friends—you respect their decisions even when they don't align with your own. Honoring others means following the advice of those placed over us and allowing ourselves to be guided by them. Sometimes it's more important to seek peace by letting people know how much you value who they are in your business or personal

> *Honoring others means following the advice of those placed over us.*

life. I applied this same principle to my stepchildren. When I changed my attitude toward them and started valuing them in my life, our relationship changed for the better.

Tony Jeary, a speaker and Christian author, says, "Let people win." It's amazing how much more profitable your transactions will be when you place the accomplishments and abilities of another person to win over your own desire.

This commandment teaches us to submit to authority by honoring others. Have you ever met someone with a rebellious, selfish spirit? Some people rebel just for the sake of it! When we rebel against the authority God has placed in our lives, we forgo an incredible blessing of God's protection and guidance. When we rebel against our bosses, managers, or companies, we lose respect for ourselves. No one wants to be around a rebel who is continually divisive, bitter, argumentative, or sarcastic. Do you display any of those traits? If so, then stop it today! You are only hurting yourself.

Submitting to authority says a tremendous amount about your character. When you have a heart that is willing to submit, you understand that authority isn't about perfection or allowing yourself to be a doormat. Submitting to authority is about honoring another, which means you're not seeking to find fault in others, but you're seeking, their highest good over your own wishes and desires. In addition, when you have authority over others it's about seeking their best too, which gives you a greater responsibility.

Recently, I had an experience in which this principle literally saved me from a nasty accident. I have been riding a bicycle since I was four-years-old, and I have never worn a helmet. The freedom of pumping and gliding has been my favorite form of exercise for years. We live near a golf course, and in the cool of the evening, I often take my bike out on the golf-course path. The wind in my hair, the exhilaration of the workout, and the music in my earphones produce a wonderful feeling and some of my most joyful alone times.

One day, my husband, mindful of my safety, asked me to purchase a helmet. "No way!" I argued. "I am not going to wear such a cumbersome thing like a helmet while I ride. You are stifling my freedom and one of the very things I love to do. I've ridden a bike my entire life and have never fallen. I refuse to wear one!" I was defiant. Finally he stopped asking me. I thought I won the argument, and the matter was dropped.

Within a few weeks, while walking through our garage, I noticed a helmet attached to my bike. It was one of those moments when I realized I had no choice but to honor his wishes. He never said a word about it again, but the message was clear, and I knew I had to comply. Of course,

I complained and moaned about the "hat-hair" that the helmet would give me and how I hated putting it on my head. He would just look at me and smile.

But I started wearing the helmet and found it was not as bad as I had first thought. A few months passed, and I decided to go for an evening ride. My husband was not home, and as I started to take off, I thought, *He will never know if I don't wear the helmet.* For a brief moment, the thought of not wearing the helmet was tempting, but wanting to honor his wishes became more important than my desire for independence. Once I began my ride, it only took a few minutes to build up my speed and take a turn on a downgrade. I did not realize it, but my tire caught in some cut grass as I made the turn, and my bike slipped out from under me. The fall was nasty, but what was worse is that my head smashed against the concrete pavement. If it had not been for the helmet, I would have sustained a serious head injury. When I called my husband on my cell phone, crying with pain, his first question was, "Were you wearing the helmet?"

Honor involves searching for the best in every situation and finding solutions for dealing with difficult bosses or people who have authority over us. When we submit to a person in a position of authority, we give respect and honor to that person. When we have authority over others, we should exhibit humility without arrogance in all that we do, think, or say to honor those under us.

> *Exhibit humility without arrogance in all that we do, think, or say.*

One couple shared with me their strategy for honoring each other. They avoid bringing annoyances up at the moment they first get irritated. Instead, they write the annoyance down (without telling the other about it), pray about it, and think about the importance of not having it become a divisive obstacle in their marriage. Then they ask God to change or eliminate that behavior in the other person or change their frustration with it. They are honoring one another by not bringing every single grievance out into the open.

Are you tearing down or building up relationships? You can tweak that type of strategy a bit to fit your lifestyle. It's about honoring the other person by building up the area in which they are lacking instead of tearing them down. Respect both your peers and foes, and give honor to your employer. Treat your support staff with dignity and value them.

What does that mean? It means choose your words carefully. Remember that words build up or destroy others. Discipline your thoughts and refrain from speaking everything that enters your mind. Identify ways in which you can praise and honor those around you. When speaking to people about areas in which they need to improve, use words that honor them without pulling them down—and always do it in private. A gentle touch can go a long way. Lift them up; don't seek to point out their faults. Be a true leader in word and deed. Give your team your vision and strategy—don't give them tasks without letting them know why they are doing something. When you make a decision to commend others and bring them joy and honor instead of treating them with judgment and criticism, you will get a more positive outcome.

> *Identify ways in which you can praise and honor those around you.*

Embracing authority might require a twist in your thinking. You might need to train your thoughts and heart to accept authority and submit to those in positions of authority. The outcome will bring honor and respect to you. Embrace it!

Questions to Ponder and Action to Take

1. Do you have a problem with authority? If so, what can you do to change your thinking about it? If you need to make amends with someone in authority over you, plan how you will approach that person.

2. Are you so determined to prove your point at times that nothing will stop you? Is there someone you need to apologize to for your bad behavior? If so, plan what you will say.

3. Is there someone in your life right now whom you need to value and honor? Make a conscious effort to begin doing so.

Commandment 6

Forgive and Let It Go

To forgive is to stop holding resentment toward another. There is emotional relief when we forgive someone for a past hurt that resulted in deep emotional wounds. Forgiveness is the most powerful weapon we have for our own well-being. By harboring anger or resentment, we keep our emotions in chains that debilitate our mental and physical health. Anger and bitterness hold hostage any good intention we might have toward another person and prevent us from being free to love. By refusing to forgive a wrong, we are the ones who end up being damaged the most.

It's no wonder that this commandment places such a high level of importance in God's eyes. In His sixth commandment, "You must not murder," He is simply telling us to forgive and let it go. Murder is the physical act, but, let's face it, holding anger in your heart can be as damaging to your spirit as actually following through with an act of violence. The act itself is horrific, but how many times have we played out such hate in our minds? Transferring this commandment to everyday living requires us to simply let go and let God take care of the situation. It's the art of practicing instant reconciliation.

The character of God can be summed up in three words: redemption, restoration, and reconciliation. This is how God treats us in our relationship with Him, and He desires that we should interact with others in the same way. Think about it—if you wanted to redeem a relationship with someone who offended you in the past, the best approach would be to let go of the past offense and attempt to restore and reconcile the relationship. Rebuild and take the higher ground by forgiving them, whether they have asked you to or not. By holding a grudge, the poison of bitterness and unforgiveness starts to creep into every aspect of your life.

It's easy to spot unforgiveness in people because their anger displays itself in so many aspects of their lives. We have all been at family gatherings over a holiday when a hurtful word is spoken, and the next thing you know, there is a family argument. Harboring anger toward others, especially toward the person who offended you, is destructive to your legacy and mental well-being.

> *The character of God can be summed up in three words: redemption, restoration, and reconciliation.*

On the other hand, if you have offended someone and have come to realize your offense, then you should attempt to restore the relationship immediately. If that person cannot accept your apology, then she must deal with her own inadequacies. But you have taken the higher road, and, in so doing, you will sustain better mental health and enjoy more happiness.

Burned in Business

A number of years ago, through some of my business connections, I was presented an opportunity that would have brought my corporation the largest account we had ever seen. It was quite a process and took several years. We pulled together a team of knowledgeable salespeople and presented a securities product to my client on a national basis. I personally had worked on the project for more than two years while maintaining my book of business in property and casualty insurance. I was consumed with selling this securities product and studied hard to obtain my securities license for this endeavor. The project had the potential to bring me financial security; it was that big.

However, unknown to me, my corporation and some of my team members were out of compliance. With securities regulations being so tight in today's fraudulent society, this was disastrous. After two years of giving my all to the task, it was closed down in just a few days without any notice to me from my superiors. My client notified me that our website had been shut down and wanted to know what was happening. I was humiliated and embarrassed in front of my client and was filled with disdain and anger toward my corporation.

I could not believe that it was over, just like that, after two years of working intently on the project, flying all over the country, meeting with many people, having my client do on-site visits at our corporate office in New York, and studying for my securities license for dozens of hours. I was devastated, and I fumed at the people who let me down, including my own company for not monitoring things more closely to prevent noncompliance.

I did not realize how angry I was until one day, while driving home from work, I started to fantasize about how to bring a lawsuit against everyone. And my fantasies about what I wanted to do to everyone personally did not stop there. It's interesting how anger can change a fairly passive person into an aggressive warrior even if it happens only in the mind. One day during my commute home, I was fuming over these events when God got my attention. It occurred to me that my anger was eating me up inside and starting to impact my health and personal life.

I was reminded of something that tweaked my thinking. A few months earlier, while traveling in Oregon to conduct presentations to the client, I had met a woman who was a writer and speaker. She was staying at the same hotel as my team and me in Bend, Oregon. She was speaking to a group of women while we were conducting our presentation at the same hotel. After spending some of my free time with her, I realized I wanted to do what she was doing instead of selling a securities product. I had always wanted to write a book. She encouraged and inspired me to just start writing. I went back to my hotel room that night and started writing my first book. It was as simple as just writing out my thoughts in a journal, but her encouragement changed my life.

So on the evening when I was driving home from work, and my anger toward my corporation was boiling inside me, I felt that inner voice remind me that meeting the writer had motivated me to begin writing my first book. And it occurred to me that this might not have happened if I had not gone through the launch of this product and traveled around the country for it. Even if the project never got off the ground, doing the presentations all over Oregon resulted in my meeting this writer friend and receiving her encouragement to start writing. Many times, failing at something gets our attention and changes the direction we meant to take. Sometimes it's the process of failure that gets our attention and initiates a change in our lives.

What I realized that evening is that the business trip to Oregon opened my eyes to what I really wanted to be doing with my life—working as an inspirational writer and conference speaker. My passion had changed, and I had not realized it until that moment in the car. So on that drive home, after giving it some consideration, I transformed my mindset and turned my anger into praise and thankfulness for this revelation of understanding. I asked God to forgive me for holding such anger toward my coworkers and my corporation. On that drive home, I let it all go, and instead of walking in the front door of my home to greet my family with the anger still seething within me, I was free from the bondage it had over me, and I had a new perspective on what I wanted to do to build my legacy.

We are taught to have a merciful heart by forgiving others instead of seeking revenge. It was Christ who expounded upon this command in Matthew 5. God will judge not only our external actions but also the feelings we harbor in our hearts. Our angry words and thoughts commit murder inwardly without any physical act (Matthew 5:21–26). Harboring anger makes us just as guilty in God's eyes as it could in our own eyes or others' eyes. By having a repentant heart and releasing the anger, we become better people. Forgiving in the midst of a desire to lash back allows you to move forward with your legacy.

I recently had a conversation with a client who is a friend, too. He went through a nasty divorce in which his wife walked out on him and their children for another man. He shared with me a realization he had after jogging in the hills by his home. He said he stopped and acknowledged his alone-

Forgiving allows you to move forward with your legacy.

ness in the wilderness. He took a rest and meditated on the hurtful events of his life. Suddenly, he felt the hand of God wiping his tears away and telling him to let it go. That moment changed everything for him. He was able to forgive his wife and let it go. What a liberating experience it was for him because he gave the anger and bitterness to God and let it go.

Sometimes it takes a supernatural act of God to help us forgive what we formerly thought was an unpardonable offense. Such was the case for this client and for Reaksa Himm.

A Story of Forgiveness

In 1977, fourteen-year-old Reaksa Himm was dumped into an open grave in the "killing fields" of Cambodia. The Khmer Rouge soldiers had left him for dead with thirteen members of his family in an open grave while they massacred additional, innocent villagers. He was able to slip into the jungle and eventually escaped to a refugee camp. As he watched his sister and mother being killed, he swore with a vengeance that he would hunt down his family's killers.

After five excruciating years in a horrific refugee camp, spending hours each day fantasizing about how he would torture and kill the murderers, he finally found his way to Canada. There he had a personal encounter with Jesus Christ and experienced God's love and mercy. It took him years to realize that his vengeful heart was only destroying his physical, mental, and spiritual growth. He had become the prisoner of his own hateful emotions and, in fact, had become the very person he despised. When he was finally able to track down his family's killers, instead of extracting vengeance he was able to truly forgive them. Through his forgiveness, he was able to shake their hands and let them know of God's mercy and love. Today he is a missionary in Cambodia, and he founded the UK-based charity called The Forgiveness Project. He has written several books about his spiritual journey.

God will always want restoration and reconciliation in all of our relationships, no matter how egregious the offense. The essence of God is always to grant mercy to us, and He calls us to emulate that characteristic and grant mercy to others. God's character is merciful, and He expects the same from us in all situations, no matter how serious the offense we experienced.

> *God will always want restoration and reconciliation in all of our relationships.*

It does not mean that justice should not prevail, but it does mean that we need to forgive others, both inwardly and outwardly, for offenses. Many of us have seen bitter old people who are so angry with the world that they have lost the ability to be civil. When I see someone like this, my first thought is, *What happened in her past that made her this bitter?*

The core root of bitterness is unforgiveness. Bitter people are easy to spot because they behave in an argumentative and harsh manner. If they could see their severe treatment of others played back to them at the end of each day, they probably would be embarrassed by their actions.

Harboring anger and bitterness is destructive. It creates in us a quality that will be unpleasant to others. If we carry such negative emotions with us as we grow older, the anger will only grow deeper. We need to forgive and let the anger go.

Questions to Ponder and Action to Take

1. Is there someone in your life now whom you need to forgive? Start by writing that person a letter.

2. Have you allowed your past negative childhood experiences to impact your life today? Do you still hold on to the anger? Make a conscious effort to let it go.

3. Do you hold grudges and always want revenge when someone hurts you? Take a different approach—forgive them.

Commandment

7

Be Loyal

LOYALTY IS A LOST virtue in our culture today, probably because its very existence requires something from us that costs time, money, and/or commitment. By nature, humans have a tendency to want to take the easy way and avoid obligation and allegiance. Loyalty requires us to be faithful and willing to persevere, no matter the cost. It forces us to go against our natural tendency, which is to run away from our problems or indulge in self-gratification. Loyalty requires us to be steadfast and true to ourselves, to others, and to God. It is a character quality everyone should hold, but unfortunately it is sadly lacking in our society today.

Loyalty is one of the most important qualities a person can possess at home and in business. The workforce is composed of many different cultures and people. Our culture says, "Just do it" or "If it feels good, do it," but living a principled life requires much more than following society's lead. Webster's dictionary defines loyalty as an unswerving allegiance and faithfulness to a cause or ideal. Do you have allegiance to your company, family, or friends? Even animals display loyalty and develop allegiance toward their clan; in fact, many animal species mate for life.

Think about all the endeavors you've been involved with in the past. No matter who your friends and coworkers are or what titles they hold, if they're not loyal, you won't trust or value them as true friends or coworkers. Loyalty in the home and loyalty in the workplace go hand in hand. There is a reason that God places this as one of the ten most important commandments, and He shows us its importance by stating, "You shall not commit adultery" (Deuteronomy 5:18). Loyalty in your marriage correlates to every aspect of your life. If you are not a loyal spouse, are you also not a loyal friend or employee? Can people trust or depend on you? Are you able to keep from gossiping or putting others down to gain approval?

This commandment teaches us about the sanctity of marriage and the importance of preserving relationships by being faithful in them. God weighs our character by our capacity to keep commitments. God established the marriage vow which is a covenant (promise) before Him between a man and

> *Loyalty in your marriage correlates to every aspect of your life.*

a woman. God established it from the beginning when He created man and woman to become one flesh. It holds great importance to God and to us because it reveals our true character as evidenced by our ability to honor obligations. Christ elaborated on this commandment by saying that in lusting for another, we have committed the act of adultery (Matthew 5:28). He went on to state that our best defense is to cut lust out of our lives so that we don't fall into temptation.

In the movie *Fireproof*, the main character, played by Kurt Cameron, attempts to recapture his wife's heart by taking a sledgehammer to his computer because he has a problem with internet pornography. The only way he can prove his loyalty to their marriage is to destroy the very thing that prevents her from believing him. It is a poignant scene in the film that leaves the viewer with an understanding that sometimes it takes a radical action to make a change. What would it take to prove your commitment to a person or a cause?

Self-Control—A Key to Loyalty

Possessing the character quality of loyalty prompts us to have complete self-control over our words, bodies, and minds. A rigid and unyielding denial of self to obtain moral sanctity begins in our minds. Self-control extends to the workforce as well because many temptations exist in the business environment that extend into other areas of our lives. For example, in the workplace there will be temptations to steal, embezzle, gossip, take credit for work done by others, undermine the work of others while advancing your own interests, or even the temptation to seek romance. Let me explain that last one.

Some people meet their mates at work. However, that's not the place to start a romance. I know this might be controversial, but it ultimately changes the atmosphere of what's supposed to occur at the office, which is work. If you are single, it's a compromise to seek love in the workplace when there are many married men who could be tempted. Office romances are often a mess and usually end with one person losing his or her job.

I love the scene in *A Few Good Men* in which Tom Cruise's character very quietly asks Demi Moore's character to stop wearing perfume because they are working so closely together on the case. The perfume was distracting him, and she was totally unaware of it.

Are women in the workplace unaware of how they're dressing or behaving? Is it a blind spot that we choose to ignore? We all have blind spots—those areas of life in which we just can't see how others perceive us. Blind spots in your life, in our culture, and in your character need to be brought to light. Awareness is the only way to transform your legacy into something of value that can last for decades. I was able to do it, and so can you!

Unfortunately, in the workplace today many women are sending the wrong message and possibly causing some good married men to stumble. Women hold the key to their own business and personal success—femininity, and many of us use it to our advantage, but at what price?

I once heard someone say that a woman sets the tone of a culture and that men just follow what the woman allows. I believe that's true. What are we allowing in our lives, and what sort of standards are we are setting for the workplace? Are we leaving a legacy of right behavior and passing it on to the next generation? Or are we compromising our values to fit the culture?

Joyce Meyer, a well-known Bible teacher and author, says that women are the thermostat in their homes. I believe that the temperature we set establishes the heat, or the way men behave in the workplace as well. Why not start to raise your standards by becoming a principled person?

How is a man supposed to concentrate or turn away when sexuality and cleavage are continually thrust in his face? What most women don't realize is that for us sexual arousal involves a process of enticement, but for a man to become aroused, all we have to do is brush by him—hence the distraction caused by Demi Moore's character with her perfume.

In many ways, women can be the role models for guiding men into right behavior. But somewhere along the way, we have lost the power to influence honorable behavior and perhaps our ability to leave a positive legacy. Have we compromised who we were made to be by misplacing our priorities and missing the opportunity to influence people for the better? It doesn't have to be that way. We can quit dressing provocatively, gossiping, and bending the truth for our personal gain. We can do better. We can leave a positive legacy for the next generation to follow and develop loyalty in our character.

Recently, I had a brief encounter with a young woman in an elevator. The encounter left me wondering about her clothing and her intentions as a professional, business woman! As she conversed on her cell phone with her earpiece, her demeanor was all business. You've seen that type before. They're everywhere. Maybe at one point or another, you've been one. Mobile devices help us do business everywhere—the coffee shop, the doctor's office, and in the confined space of an elevator.

As I observed this woman, I noticed that she carried her briefcase in one hand and her phone in the other. Her face displayed the intensity of the conversation as she attempted to obtain an order from her client. If I were blind, I would have pictured her in a business suit. I would've imagined her to be either an attorney or a corporate sales manager, based on her conversation. Her voice and demeanor were firm and distinctly professional; however, her attire was that of a professional by night. Have you ever seen something that's such a dichotomy you can't wrap your brain around it? What the heck was she thinking when she got dressed that morning? It appeared that her goal was to entice someone with her sexuality rather than project professionalism and a business demeanor.

This smart, savvy, sharp businesswoman wore a very short, tight skirt with a blouse that revealed quite a large amount of cleavage. The contrast between her demeanor and her attire was startling. Her outfit was something you'd see a woman wear in a nightclub, yet it was only 10 a.m. I had to restrain myself from saying something to her. If I'd been her client, I would have been put off, discouraged, and distracted by her attire. It's kind of like listening to a speaker but hearing nothing she says because you are so focused on her large earrings. If I were her colleague or friend, I would've said, "You don't have to dress like that to call attention to yourself. Your professional demeanor says how successful you are, and dressing for a night out only calls attention to the fact that you use sex for attention." Or maybe this: "You have so much more in you. You're selling yourself short by dressing that way."

I held my tongue at that moment, but it caused me to realize that someone needs to start saying something! As women, we have so much more to offer at home and in the workplace. If you want true success, make a statement with your life, not with an outward appearance of sexuality. Anyone can look

> *Dress for success professionally without looking like a showgirl.*

like a hooker standing on a street corner, but a woman of dignity will make the effort to dress for success professionally without looking like a showgirl.

Be loyal to yourself and your employer by not looking for romance in the office.

What Is Success?

This is a book about success, and I think it is important to define it. I believe that no matter what you do, it's important to define success in terms of being authentic with yourself and centered in your walk with God. We seek human success, but what if that is not God's motive? God calls us to follow Him in faith, and the path He wants us to follow might not be the outcome we've built up in our minds. As our Creator, God is sovereign over the entire universe. He has set a standard for our success that is not that hard to follow. God's measurement of success is instilled in relationships and how much loyalty we display towards others. Are we honoring our self, Him and those we work with in the process of seeking achievement, by being loyal?

My friend felt that God called him to run for Congress, but he lost the election. Despite the outcome, he felt that God had clearly called him to run. For him, maybe it wasn't all about winning; maybe it was about being faithful to the call to see what inner strength he had to trust God. Success for you might not be to amass riches. If you stay true to who you are and develop your character with honor, dignity, and loyalty, then you have found true success.

Make a Statement with Your Life, Not Your Body

A girl who once worked for me had a giant dragon tattoo on her back, and she made sure that she showed it every day by wearing short tops. Did it affect her productivity? Maybe not, but it certainly affected my opinion of her and probably impacted her opportunity for promotion. If she was hoping to make a favorable impression, the exact opposite of what she was attempting to achieve happened—I thought less of her because she felt it was more important to dress to show the tattoo than to dress in a professional manner appropriate for an office setting.

Piercings and tattoos can be a turnoff to a boss. It's your choice, but ultimately it's important to think about your professional goals. Anyone can get pierced or tattooed, but not everyone has the creativity and skills you possess. Shine in those areas. Remember, what seems like a cool thing today to gain your friends' attention may not be so cool five years from now. Learn to be loyal to yourself and to value your body.

A while ago, I met a girl at the Clinique makeup counter in a department store who had long sleeves on during the summer. She was very professional, quite attractive, and a great salesperson. I noticed that when her sleeve lifted, there was ink on her wrist. "Do you have a tattoo?" I asked.

She looked down with disgust. "I do," she said. "I went through a rebellious phase when I was a teenager. I have tattoos all over my body, and I regret that I am covered in them." She continued, "I wish I could tell every young girl out there to think twice before they do something so permanent to their bodies. I truly regret what I did, and I have no one to blame but myself."

I'm not saying that tattoos and piercings are bad. I'm saying that you should think about your life before you do something like make a permanent mark on your body that you might regret years later. Learn how to think of the big picture, which includes God's world, not just your own. Learn how to be a loyal friend and coworker, and give up your selfish desires. This might mean you have to set aside your desire to wear a miniskirt at work or to show some cleavage. If you learn to project professionalism and dress to succeed, achievement will follow.

We have all heard the saying "dress for success." There is truth in this statement. When you project success in how you dress and behave, success follows you.

The Power of Self-Awareness

Self-examination is essential in the process of developing loyalty to God and others. There is nothing mystical or magical about it. You just need to take an honest look at yourself as God sees you and desires you to become. If you're unclear about how to proceed, ask God to show you the blind spots. The actions you take call attention to your motives. The things we meditate on and think about become the actions we take. If we have darkness in our hearts, our actions reveal that darkness. For instance, if you are jealous of another individual and you gossip about her, the action of gossiping is an outward revelation of your inner darkness.

I was completely unaware of the intense feelings of jealousy I harbored toward a woman I knew. I decided not to invite her to a specific event in my life. Later on, when I thought about my actions, I realized that I had not invited her to the event because of the darkness in my own heart toward her. It manifested itself in my actions after I was put in charge of coordinating the event and inviting people to attend. By not inviting her, I was, in essence, saying, "You're not wanted here." What a cruel thing to do to someone. It would have been one thing to not invite her because there was no more

When we allow the conviction in our heart to have its way, freedom becomes a reality.

room, but to do it purely out of jealousy was wrong. After I realized what I had done, I repented and asked God to cleanse me of my jealousy and hostility toward this person.

I didn't repent out of sacrifice but out of obedience. I wanted a clear conscience. This type of freedom results in joy. When we allow the conviction in our heart to have its way, freedom becomes a reality. Being loyal to yourself is the first step in building the legacy you long to make.

Questions to Ponder and Action to Take

1. To what extent do you consider yourself to be loyal to your family and friends? What steps can you take to change your thinking so that you can become a more loyal person?

2. Assess yourself with regard to your relationships. Give yourself an evaluation of loyalty to your friends. Are you a loyal friend and employee? What can you do better?

3. Write out your thoughts on loyalty and determine to develop this trait in your character.

Commandment

8

Give of Yourself

GIVING OF YOURSELF IS the ultimate sacrifice because it requires something of you. As difficult as this may seem at first, it eventually produces great abundance of personal character and inner joy. It forces you to offer something precious: your time, your money, or your effort for a worthy cause. The opposite of stealing is giving. It means going the second mile and doing much more than necessary when there is an opportunity. When you have a servant attitude and give of yourself, you will derive benefits that far outweigh the sacrifice.

I have tried to maintain a servant attitude as I implement my business practices. For example, I make a presentation to potential clients several months before their insurance was due to be renewed. I would show my worth and value to their business by managing their claims and acting as if I was already their broker. My competitors never offered to do work for the prospect before they made any revenue on it. It always took the business owner by surprise that someone would show their worth before making any money. A few times, potential clients took advantage of me and used my expertise, but nine times out of ten, I would get the account.

The "Also Principle"

My friend, Devi Titus, teaches this concept as the "Also Principle," and it can apply to every aspect of your life. In her teaching, she uses the story of Rebecca in the Bible. The servant of Abraham was looking for a wife for Isaac, Abraham's son, so the servant was sent to the country of Abraham's birth to find a wife for Isaac. In the story, Rebecca saw the servant under a tree needing a drink. She did not know that the servant had prayed to God about which girl to choose as Isaac's wife. The divine answer came to him in the form of instructions to notice how the young woman would respond to his request for water. Not only did Rebecca offer the servant water; she "also" provided water for his camels, which was not an easy task.

A small herd of camels could drink dozens of gallons of water after a long ride. By offering to feed the camels water, she was telling Abraham's servant she would go to the well and retrieve the needed water and carry it over in pots to his camels. It was a difficult job for any young girl, but by doing this, her character was revealed. Abraham knew his son's wife would have to be a very special person with unique qualities to become the mother of a nation.

Rebecca went the extra mile in also providing water for his camels, and she was rewarded for her effort—she became Isaac's wife. The "Also Principle" can apply to everything you think, say, or do in your home or office. It's a marvelous principle around which to build your life. By offering to provide water for the camels, Rebecca displayed a caring and giving spirit. Her character reflected an inner beauty.

Years after I heard Devi teach this principle, we were in a public restroom together. She was cleaning up the water and paper towels around the sink, a mess that someone else had left. I laughed because I knew that she was applying the "Also Principle" to a very small aspect of her life—cleaning up after herself and also cleaning up after others so that the area would be clean for the next person. She performed a small act of kindness, but it is a powerful principle to apply in your life.

Give of yourself in time and effort to make things better for those who succeed you. Maybe there will be no immediate benefit, but in time you will become a better person.

The eighth commandment in the Bible says, "You shall not steal" (Deuteronomy 5:19). It might seem clear, but what if we look at the larger picture of not stealing? It could mean that not only should we refrain from stealing another person's possessions, but we should also not steal another person's love, family, or destiny, either. People who steal are indulging their selfish desires. We must let go of our selfish desires and give of ourselves in all aspects of our lives—that is the essence of God. Cheating others of their material possessions, time, or money is ultimately stealing from God. Have you ever thought about it from that perspective?

> *Give of yourself in time and effort to make things better for those who succeed you.*

A wonderful teaching came from Christ when He washed the apostles' feet (John 13:5). In those days, people wore sandals on dusty roads and paths. The feet were considered the filthiest part of a person's body. A servant was the only person who washed his master's feet, so when Christ washed the apostles' feet, it was a true demonstration of His character.

This story exemplifies the spirit of giving of oneself to another. By being a servant to all, we are giving to the fullest extent, thus fulfilling this commandment. God intended the motive of our hearts to be what is best for others, not ourselves. If we give anything less than that, we are stealing from others and from God.

Called to Motherhood

This principle presented itself to me when my husband and I had an opportunity to raise his two nieces. When I decided to pursue a career in business, I made a conscious decision to not have children. This decision came about due to my many babysitting experiences, which made me realize that having children is a lot of hard work. In fact, I believe it is the hardest job a person can take on. I decided to make my life easier and not have children. But God had another plan for my life.

While my husband and I were dating, his brother passed away, and his wife became unfit to raise their two daughters. We supported them financially for several years after we were married, and that worked for a while. However, within a few years after being married, we got a call from a case worker asking if it mattered to us that my husband's two nieces were in foster care. That call changed our lives forever.

Within a few short months, I became a mother for the first time in my life. What a transition my life took on from the very first day! I was no longer thinking only about my business and own desires for my marriage. I now had to be concerned about the welfare of two little girls. We used to eat out often, but I had to start cooking and making sure the girls ate plenty of fruits and vegetables. I also had to make sure they did their homework, and I screened what they watched on television. Instantly, my life changed forever.

It was not easy because the girls were suffering much emotional distress as a result of their alcoholic, abusive mother. Despite many difficulties, we continued to give of ourselves, and today we have two beautiful young women in our lives who are making a positive impact on the world.

Many people have told us that the girls are so blessed, but I can honestly say that my husband and I are the ones who are blessed. God used two little girls to teach me what it means to give and love sacrificially.

In business, this taught me the same concept. By going the extra mile and giving my best to my clients, people usually entrusted me with all their insurance lines. I have a strong client retention rate. Some of my clients have stayed with me for more than twenty years. People will see your value when you put their needs first.

For me, this impacted me when I began my career in insurance and became focused on a large account involving workers' compensation. When I first visited this particular client, he barely had the time to see me. In fact, he had cancelled the first appointment with me. When I finally got a few minutes with him, he initially stated that he had only ten to fifteen minutes to talk. Nearly two hours later, I still had his attention, and I was able to show him the evidence of work I had done for other clients. He had a long relationship with his broker, and it was a hard sell to convince him to leave that broker and allow me to become his new broker. The final aspect, that convinced him to switch brokers, was some work I had done on his claims prior to getting the account. He was so impressed by the work I had done that he gave me the order without hesitation at that point.

Showing people your value before you start the job gives you an edge over your competitors that will leave a lasting impression. There will be times when that does not work, but don't let someone's ignorance stop you from going the extra mile. Putting yourself out there and giving of your time and talents can never hurt your career. I always believed that, when a prospect did not

> *Take time today to do something for someone.*

purchase their insurance from me, it was more their loss than mine.

Prioritizing your time and realizing what really matters is the first step in learning this commandment. Are you making time for others in order to pour into their lives something of value? Or are you so intent on the task at hand that you forget how to treat people with dignity and respect and make time for them? Giving of yourself speaks volumes about the type of person you have become. Take time today to do something for someone without any expectation of a return benefit.

Questions to Ponder and Action to Take

1. When was the last time you volunteered for a worthy cause? Make a commitment to initiate a difference in someone else and to treat people with dignity and respect. Volunteer at the Boys and Girls Club or some other organization.

2. Have you ever purchased something for someone even though it wasn't a special occasion? Plan to do that this week.

3. Remember how special someone made you feel when they gave you their time and attention? Do the same for another person this week.

Commandment 9

Be Authentic and Truthful

To be authentic means to be genuine, to not present a counterfeit version of yourself to the world. When you are authentic and truthful, your intentions are sincere in any situation, thus validating your character to others. Being authentic is being true to yourself and not allowing lies, corruption, falsehood, or even exaggeration to be a part of your life. Authentic living allows you to be a realistic rendering of who you are before God, yourself, and others without any false pretenses.

To live a life of true success and grow the legacy you desire, you must be authentic. It is not an option. That means being real with God and being able to look at yourself in the mirror and honestly evaluate who that person is whose image is reflected back to you. If you are authentic, you do not pretend that everything is fine when it isn't. And you do not harbor pain and anger deep within your soul while portraying a false pretense of happiness to those around you. The anger will come out at some point when you least expect it. You have to know yourself as you were created and treat others with the same authentic genuineness. When you display honesty, you are trustworthy and can be counted on to respond appropriately to the reality of the situation and the facts at hand.

Intentional efforts to be authentic and truthful will shape you into a strong woman with a backbone to stand on your principles. You are to be a light in the darkness and exude truth and honesty. How can you be light if you have gray areas that mask the truth? Light penetrates dark, but dark cannot overcome light. Think about it. When it's nighttime and you turn a lamp on, the darkness is dispersed. We are called to live a lifestyle that illuminates truth and authentic living. We are to disperse the darkness in people's hearts by being real.

Honesty is another virtue that seems to be scarce among those who are looking for success. People seem to speak lies so casually today that they start believing their own rewritten history as the truth. When are we going to start being authentic and honest with each other? We need to stop masquerading as authentic people when, in fact, our conversations are filled with falsehood and exaggeration.

It reminds me of the story of the CEO who began looking for his replacement. He was unsure which of his children should take over his company, so instead he decided to open the job up to all of his managers. At the beginning of the year, he gave each of his managers a

Exude truth and honesty.

seed, and he asked them to plant it in soil and nurture it to full maturity. At the end of the year, all but one of the managers, who were vying for the job of CEO, showed up with beautiful plants and trees in their pots. That one manager had a seed that never grew into anything, and he was embarrassed to bring it forward at the end of the year, but he did. When the CEO saw the dead plant, he chose that manager as his successor. You see, he had boiled each seed so that it would not produce any vegetation, and that manager was the only one who was truthful. As embarrassing and difficult as it was to be honest, this manager had decided to take the higher road and be authentic. He faced what he thought would be complete humiliation. As a result, he was awarded the job, because of his honesty and integrity.

Are you willing to be honest even to the point of embarrassment and pain? Most of the time, we would rather tell a lie than the truth because it might make us look bad or we might have some explaining to do because of our actions. I would rather have my staff come forward with the truth about a mistake they have made with a client than to cover it up, only to be found out later.

This has happened several times with some of my past employees, and in each case, I lost the client because I was given misinformation. Ultimately, the employees lost their jobs, too, because I could no longer rely on or trust the information they provided me. An employer must be able to trust the work you do and the person you are; otherwise, they will be spending too much time checking your work. If these former employees had been honest from the start about an error, I might have been able to retain the client. Most importantly, I needed to know that I had someone

I could count on who had my back covered, someone who would be honest with me and let me know the truth. Mistakes provide opportunities for teachable moments, and we can grow and increase our knowledge from them, but covering up an error changes the mistake into deceit.

When someone admits his or her mistakes, it is much easier to forgive that person than someone who intentionally lies and tries to hide their mistakes. It is only human to make mistakes, which can be pardoned, but when someone tries to hide their errors, they often go all out to defend their actions. How can people find forgiveness if they will not admit their errors? This is why it is important to be honest with ourselves and with others.

When you go through trials and tribulations, be honest with yourself. Look in the mirror and ask yourself, "Am I giving my all? Am I invested with this project and with God one hundred percent? Have I committed myself to building a foundation of following God's precepts?"

Where you invest your time and thoughts will be reflected in what you become. The world is full of nominal people who never accom-

Covering up an error changes the mistake into deceit.

plish anything with their lives, let alone leave a legacy. The reality is that most clients or bosses know when you are lying and cheating them, and even if you win in the short term, you will always end up paying the piper in the end.

Be willing to admit your mistakes to your family, employer, and clients. People would rather have honesty than have others around them attempting to cover up their mistakes. The ninth commandment says, "You shall not bear false witness against your neighbor" (Deuteronomy 5:20). In other words, we should not lie about people and about our circumstances. Those who do not bear a false witness are authentic and live with a free conscience.

Dishonesty in the Workplace

A personal experience I had with our regional CEO a number of years ago left my entire staff disenchanted with his ability to lead. I had already suspected on many occasions that he was not an honest person, but this one event sealed it for me that he could never be trusted from his word.

We were in a sales meeting when one of my peers spoke up and complained about the lack of support our marketing manager was giving to our new business submissions. The marketing manager was a direct appointment whom our CEO had hired; he was a close personal friend of the CEO, too. Our CEO took it personally when my peer complained about the marketing manager's lack of ability to do the work we salespeople needed him to do. Instead of listening to the salesperson and agreeing to look into the matter, the CEO defended the marketing manager and his work. The CEO jumped up immediately and addressed the sales producer in a defensive, aggressive manner. He stated, "It's not like I send him off to enjoy himself at all the carrier functions, like the Masters Golf Tournament, and he becomes too busy schmoozing carriers to do the marketing work." In other words, instead of our regional CEO being a leader and investigating the matter, he took the complaint personally and manipulated the situation to make it look like the sales producer was the problem for complaining.

Before ten minutes had passed after the sales meeting, I walked into another sales producer's office to discuss a project. The marketing manager swung by to present my sales peer with a t-shirt he had purchased at the Masters Golf Tournament. Indeed, the regional CEO had just sent the marketing manager to the Masters Golf Tournament!

There was no need to tell a lie to all of us in the sales meeting. Because the CEO did not know how to tell the truth when put on the spot, he displayed openly his inability to be authentic. He lost the entire sales staff's respect that morning and soon found himself out of a job because our corporate headquarters had enough of his lies as well.

Within our inner thoughts, deception can produce a falsehood in every aspect of our lives, and many times we are unaware of it. Truthfulness and honesty create a clean conscience, which contributes to healthy living and positive relationships. Preferring truth over duplicity develops strong character and morality. Truth is the foundation of God's character. He is the absolute truth (John 14:6).

Having a clean heart before God and man will result in dependability and reliability which are characteristics that will help you build deep and abiding relationships founded on mutual trust.

Questions to Ponder and Action to Take

1. Have you ever made a mistake and tried to cover it with a lie? If so, what can you do to make amends now? Commit to taking the necessary action.

2. Are you able to assess yourself honestly and evaluate your closest relationships in light of being authentic? What can you do better, and what will you commit to changing?

3. Your true character is tested when you go through a trial. Have you recently gone through a trying time, and did you persevere with honesty? If not, how can you be more honest and authentic in the future?

10 Commandment

Find Contentment

NOTHING IN LIFE BRINGS more complete fulfillment than inner peace and contentment. Inner peace is harmony in all relationships and freedom from anxiety and fear. Contentment is a state of tranquility and freedom from wants, desires, and guilt. Having inner peace and contentment creates confidence and security and removes all doubt, fear, bitterness, and jealousy. It removes all feelings of envy and the desire to have things we do not possess. It leads to true satisfaction and joy.

It seems fitting to devote the final chapter of this book to one of the most important life principles and objectives you could ever strive for in life. You can have all of the success in the world, but it's nothing without true inner peace and contentment. In the workforce, if you don't have the quality of being fulfilled, no matter how smart or accomplished you are, you won't ever feel happy, and you won't attain true success. You will always feel an empty desire to do more, make more, and be more.

Often in the business world it's all about the next thing you can do for the corporation. You can never rest on your past accomplishments because there is always some sort of expectation to do more. Many people in the business world cannot find true contentment because their self-esteem is drawn from their business accomplishments. What most people don't realize is that, once you leave the corporate world, someone will be right behind you to take your place, and your accomplishments will be forgotten soon.

I have a neighbor who gave me a lift one day. In the few moments we drove together he shared with me his concern about the past week and how he had to work during his vacation. He was fretting that he had to spend time working while he was suppose to be taking a few days off work. I mentioned to him that work was not worth getting a heart attack over, as I discerned he was very stressed and had a lot of anxiety over his job. Our conversation led him to sharing something his mother taught him when he was young. As he shared with me her words, he was realizing her words were prophetic for this time now. When he was young and newly married with children, she had noticed that he was putting his career before his family and that concerned her.

What she said to him was true wisdom. She told him to take a bucket and fill it with water. She went on to state, if you truly thought you were worth something then put your elbow into the bucket of water. She said to him, "Now pull your elbow out of the water. Observe as the water replaces all the space your elbow takes, this is how little you will be missed in your office after you leave." Remember keeping balance in your career and home life is essential to your contentment.

Why miss out on the family reunion for the sake of your job? I once skipped a vacation with some girlfriends because I felt my client could not do without me. How silly a notion to think things will fall apart if I am not there to take care of them. I missed a fun time with friends and an opportunity to reaffirm our relationships. The good news is that it's not too late to make some changes in your lifestyle and to prioritize your relationships from this time forward.

What Is Peace?

True peace is manifested by a lack of anxiety, discontentment, and fear. It's finding an overall comfort with who you are and where you are in life. When you are at peace, you have a strong sense that you are exactly where you're supposed to be and doing what you are supposed to be doing. Peace is keeping a clear mind and not allowing negativity to be a part of your life.

I recently had a call from a young woman I know. She shared with me her intense anxiety and constant fear. She was even contemplating suicide. I had contacted her via e-mail when I read her blog on Facebook. My email prompted her to call me. She had been posting a blog on vampires and witchcraft and doing a lot of research in this area. Over a period of several conversations with me, she determined that her fearful thoughts had manifested themselves when she started doing her research for the blog. She had purchased books on vampires and witchcraft for the sake of research, but she discovered that the books were influencing her in a negative way. She also had been watching television shows and movies that enhanced her fear. Once she gave these things up, the anxious feelings and fear left her.

It's hard to find inner peace when you constantly feed your mind negative books, movies, and television shows. I cleansed our house years ago of books and movies and anything else that would impact my family in a negative or fearful way. Peace will not call itself into your life if you are constantly feeding your brain fearful thoughts and negative activity.

Eliminating Covetousness

The opposite of peace is coveting something you don't have and being discontented with your current state. Unrest comes when there's a gap between what we have and another person's possessions which we covet. Blessings beyond measure can be reached when you find satisfaction with your current situation and circumstances. Peace and contentment make one rich from within, and they will express themselves in a fulfilling lifestyle.

> *Peace and contentment make one rich from within.*

Peace and contentment are qualities you don't have to earn because they stem from appreciation and thankfulness within the heart.

The tenth commandment in the Bible, "You shall not covet your neighbor's wife" (Deuteronomy 5:21), really speaks to the heart of one's soul. When we covet anything, our souls are in a state of unrest and are never fully complete. Our flesh desires more and more.

By not coveting, we learn to find contentment. When you are content with your current circumstances, it is a marvelous state of being. Peace and tranquility become the blessing of a contented life. Coveting creates a selfish attitude that is the exact opposite of the character God desires for us. Continual desire for what we do not have will find no rest and will lure us into numerous temptations which will never bring satisfaction. What do you want that you can't have?

Finding contentment reminds me of the story of the fisherman in a tiny village in Mexico. He had a good life. He slept in late, played with his children, took siestas every day, and was able to catch enough fish each day to sell in the village and feed his family. Then one day, a tourist tasted his fish and offered to put him in business because the fisherman had a talent for finding the best fish to serve in restaurants. The tourist told him that if he worked a little harder, he could double his inventory, buy another boat, and grow his business. As he grew his business, then he could make investments and earn more money.

The fisherman looked puzzled and asked, "After I make more money, then what can I do with it?"

The tourist replied, "You will be able to relax, sleep in late, play with your children, take siestas every day, and fish when you feel like it because you will have enough money to retire on."

Sometimes we just need to look around and realize that the very thing we desire is right in front of us.

The first step toward having peace is to eliminate obsessive desires that will control you if you let them. Get rid of the desire for that job, person, or habit that is not God's perfect will for your life. If acquiring that desire makes you want to do something dishonest to get it, then it is not for you. If you obtain something by dishonest means, do you really think it will make you happy? Fulfillment comes when you work for something, and the harder you work to earn it, the more fulfilling it will be to you. Learn to be "in the moment" each day. Find happiness in the little things, and start appreciating the things you already have in your life. How many times have we let the day slip by without really appreciating what we already have—spouse, family, home, job, friends? Take time out right now to write out your many blessings, and start to appreciate them daily.

When the girls came to live with us, we started spending our weekends doing kids' sports and activities. An awful day for us at the time was taking seven little girls to Magic Mountain, which at first seemed like a good idea. It was our daughter's birthday, and she wanted to go to the theme park with her friends. While we were there, it started to rain, and a lot of the rides broke down. We would wait in line for what seemed like hours, only to find out that the ride was not working when we got to the front of the line. It was cold and rainy, and all I could think about was getting home and being warm. There was a moment when the girls were all huddled in line, and they started to pray that God would end the rain so this one ride would start to work. After a while, the line started to move, and the girls got to go on the ride. It was a precious moment, and their excitement and joy were heartwarming. Now that my youngest is an adult and has her own life with little time to spend with us, I often reflect on that day and wish I could relive it with more appreciation.

Those days are now gone. The girls are grown. They work in different areas, and they have started to build their own lives. Recently, I was recalling that memory with a young mother who was complaining about having to attend a weekend soccer match with her young son. It dawned on me that I would give anything to have those days back. Our days with loved ones disappear so quickly. If we don't find the time to really appreciate those people and events, they will slip through our fingers and be gone forever. Nothing ever stays the same. Kids grow up, and change is constant, but if we take the time to live in the moment, we might find true, inner joy.

Although my friends would laugh at this now, when I was young, I was what might be termed a "hippie." I was into organic gardening, canning my own fruits and vegetables, and baking my own bread. That life is so far removed from my corporate life today! It's hard to believe that, at one time, I would not wear makeup, but I did wear tie-dyed skirts. One thing I remember during that period in my life was the peace and tranquility I experienced in the morning with a cup of coffee while reading my Bible and looking at my garden. To sit on the back step and meditate on scripture, while enjoying the fruit of my labor from the vegetable garden, was fulfilling. I still spend each morning in scripture and meditation, but I do miss the labor of gardening in my busy life today. It was a very tranquil period of my life that brought an abundance of contentment.

When you find comfort in who you are and the person you have become, you will experience a form of contentment that cannot be purchased. True success is being a woman of depth and character, not achieving wealth.

When God is pleased with us, His favor is personified in contentment that fills our souls with complete joy. The fruit of His Spirit (love, joy, peace, patience, kindness, goodness, faithfulness, gentleness, and self-control—Galatians 5:22–23) will be manifested and enhanced by those who learn to

> *True success is being a woman of depth and character, not achieving wealth.*

find contentment in the little blessings of each day. When these fruits are demonstrated in your daily life, then you have achieved true contentment.

Questions to Ponder and Action to Take

1. What do you want that you cannot possess or achieve? Maybe it's time to reprioritize your thinking and change your mindset with regard to this desire.

2. Have you ever experienced the fruits of God's Spirit? If not, focus on experiencing and appreciating them.

3. Have you ever experienced true peace in the midst of things falling apart? If not, commit to doing so the next time you experience a difficult situation.

Conclusion

MANY TIMES IN THE workplace, circumstances can cause you to experience a crisis of belief—you are not sure where you will stand or what action you will take. The decision you make can have long-term consequences and impact your career and even your destiny.

When you know in your heart who you are and you are confident in the woman you have become, your decisions become easier. Although those decisions may be difficult at the time, they will be easier if you have determined the legacy you desire to leave. Becoming a woman of integrity establishes in your soul a deep, abiding presence of joy and peace that will affirm your stance in difficult times. The decisions you make are then grounded in wisdom and help protect your reputation and honor.

Changing your character is not an easy fix. It requires a daily determination to become a better person in your thoughts and actions. There will be times when you slip and fall, but your best defense against mistakes will be to forget your folly and move forward with determination to learn from your blunder.

It is my hope that this book will help you become more successful in your career and life as you grow to develop your moral compass and leave a legacy of a principled life.

IF YOU'RE A FAN OF THIS BOOK, PLEASE TELL OTHERS

- Write a positive review on www.amazon.com.

- Purchase additional copies to give away as gifts.

- Suggest *The Ten Commandments of Business Success for Women* to friends.

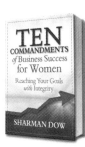

- Write about *The Ten Commandments of Business Success for Women* on your blog. Post excerpts to your social media sites such as: Facebook, Twitter, Pinterest, Instagram, etc.

- When you're in a bookstore, ask if they carry the book.

You can order additional copies of the book from my website by going to www.sharmandow.com.

Invite Sharman to your next event!

- Contact Sharman at www.sharmandow.com. and schedule her to speak at your next event or to coach you or your team.

Would you like Sharman to bring an **Empower Women's Conference** to your City?

The Empower Women's Conference will provide you with tools that will motivate you to see your current business position as an opportunity to become an architect for change and achieve personal success in the workplace and at home!

Contact us today at www.EmpowerWomensConference.com for more information.

Bring Sharman and her team to **YOU** and share the wisdom and insights of these successful business women. Motivating and equipping today's woman for tomorrow's challenges!

www.EmpowerWomensConference.com